C000077264

DRIVING SNOWDONIA

Driving Snowdonia

Richard Quine

First published in 2010

© Richard Quine

© Gwasg Carreg Gwalch 2010

ISBN: 978-1-84524-157-5

Cover design: Sian Parri

Published by Llygad Gwalch,
Ysgubor Plas, Llwyndyrys,
Pwllheli, Gwynedd, Wales, LL53 6NG,
tel: 01758 750432
fax: 01758 750438
email: gai@llygadgwalch.co.uk
internet: www.carreg-gwalch.co.uk

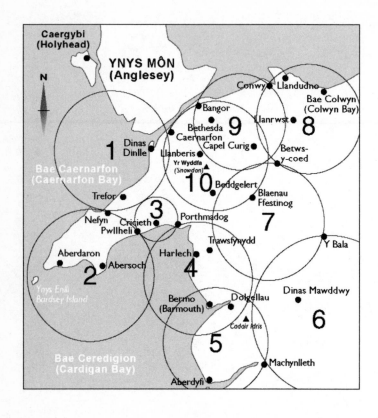

Contents

Author's Note

I sympathise with those who would like to ban or restrict cars from the more popular parts of Snowdonia, for there is no doubt that the only way to fully appreciate this beautiful area is on foot; and that the internal combustion engine has a lot for which to answer.

However, Snowdonia is a living and working area and people need their cars to go about their business. There are many of us who, like myself, through age and infirmity are no longer able to scramble up and down mountains; then there are those with disabilities, who should not be denied the right to explore the area; finally, there are those who suffer from the modern disease of 'not having enough time' to explore on foot. Whichever category you find yourself in, I hope that this book will help to broaden your knowledge of the area. The diversity of the National Park is such that it is impossible to cover all in one volume, but I hope the notes accompanying the journeys will whet your appetite to find out more – and to this end may I draw your attention to the range of informative and modestly priced books on all aspects of Wales published by Gwasg Carreg Gwalch.

Finally, may I thank the many friends and relatives who have given me the pleasure of their company over many years exploring Snowdonia – particularly my constant companion Rosie, who has covered many more miles on her four legs than I have on two! I hope you don't get lost too often following my directions, and that you are still on speaking terms with your navigator at the end of your journey, but above all please drive considerately – there may be a party of walkers round the next bend. Thank you.

Richard Quine
January 2010

Introduction

Mention 'Snowdonia' and most people think of Snowdon summit and its immediate surroundings containing the thirteen peaks over 3,000 ft (915 m). But the Snowdonia National Park, or to give it its Welsh title, Parc Cenedlaethol Eryri, formed in 1951, covers an area of 840 square miles (2,175 sq. km), stretching 50 miles (80 km) from the Dyfi estuary in the south to that of the river Conwy in the north and from Bae Ceredigion in the west to Llyn Tegid (near Bala) in the east. Llŷn, the north-western peninsula of Wales, has been included in this book because of its proximity to Snowdonia, and because its coastal scenery often includes these mountains. The book covers the county of Gwynedd, together with incursions into Powys in the south-east and Conwy in the north.

It is an area of outstanding beauty and diversity: awe-inspiring mountains, raging waterfalls, tranquil lakes, peaceful valleys, beautiful estuaries and miles of award-winning beaches. It is an area full of history from pre-Roman times to the present day – there are several prehistoric sites, early Celtic settlements, Roman forts, pilgrim churches, Welsh castles, invading army strongholds – and much, much more. For those interested in nature there are twelve National Nature Reserves and nine major sites of Special Scientific Interest (SSSIs), together with numerous opportunities for birdwatching. For those interested in matters mechanical there are six narrow gauge railways; abandoned gold, silver, copper and lead mines; and slate and granite quarries too numerous to mention.

The National Trust owns tracts of the countryside whilst CADW, the heritage organisation, looks after many historic buildings and sites.

It is accepted that the only way to fully appreciate the

countryside is by walking, but to cover such a large area on foot is well nigh impossible. Even by car you will need more than a day or two.

The format of this book is one of a chain with ten links, each of which represents a circular route round a section of the area. Since the routes are linked together the chain can be joined at any point depending on where one is staying, and take in one or more links at a time. (For some unaccountable reason the links have turned out to be in an anti-clockwise direction! Is this because we drive on the left?) Each route is about 60 miles (100 km) and, in theory, could be completed in half a day, but because of the roads chosen and allowing for stops, a full day is recommended.

Where possible, the main roads with their traffic – particularly heavy at holiday times – have been avoided in favour of 'off the beaten track' roads and lanes. In many cases these are narrow and twisting, and it could be said that they are not for faint hearted or inexperienced drivers. However, the effort is well worthwhile, for the minor roads frequently give better views of the countryside, reach more interesting places, and perhaps, more importantly, allow one to stop without finding another car on one's tail!

Two words of warning – firstly, due to the closure of many rural petrol stations it is advisable to keep a full tank, and secondly, a reminder that the police in this area are particularly keen to enforce speed limits. Having referred to the narrowness of some of the roads, all are passable with care and in surprisingly good condition. It is, however, essential to be able to reverse for possibly a considerable distance.

A good navigator is almost essential, if only to open (and close) the gates!

The opportunity has been taken to include one or two short walks in each chapter for those who welcome a chance to stretch their legs.

With a coastline 150 miles (241 km) from Colwyn Bay to Aberdyfi, it is not surprising that there have been shipwrecks – indeed hundreds of them, particularly in the days of sail. A few of the more interesting wrecks are referred to here.

Distances are approximate and are given in imperial, with metric equivalent in brackets.

The new OS Travel Map Tour 10 (1 inch to 2¾ miles – 1 cm to 1.75 km) covers the whole of north and central Wales, and is probably the most useful. For those wanting a larger scale, the OS Explorer maps OL17, OL18, OL23, 253 and 254 (2½ inches to 1 mile – 4 cm to 1 km) cover the area between them.

The rugged nature of this area has meant that in years gone by little contact was had with those beyond Offa's Dyke, and thus the Welshness of the area has been maintained for centuries. The coming of the railways in the nineteenth century and the motor car in the twentieth century changed all that, bringing in the holidaymakers, the more wealthy business commuters, and second home owners. The Welsh culture has largely survived, but the language has suffered through enforced English-only education in the nineteenth century, and the globalisation of smaller cultures in the twentieth century. At the end of the last century, Welsh-language speaker figures were on the increase, however, and the national language is now prominent on road signs, on television and all official documents. Most first-language Welsh people in this area are bilingual, but Welsh being their first language, it will be heard almost everywhere in the region. Efforts to increase the number of Welsh speakers, particularly amongst the 'incomers', is meeting with some success. As in any country, it is polite and appreciated if at least a few words are spoken in the native tongue. Half a dozen spring to mind:

Croeso	Welcome
Bore da	Good morning
Nos da	Good night
Diolch yn fawr	Thank you
Iechyd da	Good health

And to avoid embarrassment:

Dynion	Men
Merched	Women

A few more commonly heard words are given in the glossary at the end.

Throughout the book, place-names are given in Welsh with English in brackets.

For those wishing to delve more deeply into this subject read *Pronouncing Welsh Place-names* by Tony Leaver, and for more information on the meanings of Welsh place-names, *The Place-name Detective* by Anthony Lias, both published by Gwasg Carreg Gwalch.

Throughout this book, place-names are given in Welsh with English in brackets.

It is hoped that with the aid of this little look you will enjoy happy and carefree motoring.

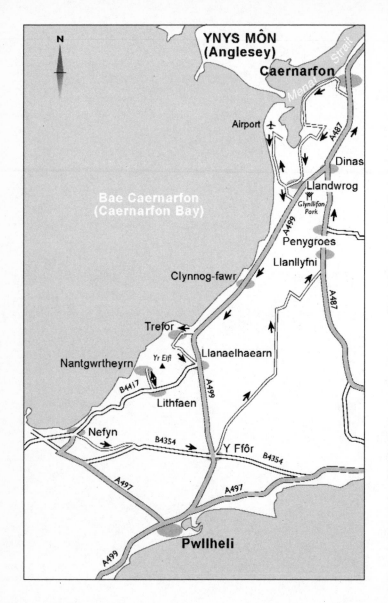

Link 1

Caernarfon – Nefyn – Caernarfon

Distance: 57 miles (91 kilometres)
Time: 2 hours plus stops

Description

This link in the chain is not actually in the Snowdonia National Park, but it covers an area of scenic and historical interest, and is therefore well worth a visit. It also joins onto the next link which covers the beautiful peninsula of Llŷn.

The route initially follows the banks of the Menai Strait with perhaps the finest view of the castle, and then follows the coastline to reminders of the area's industrial past as far as the old town of Nefyn. The return journey is through the winding lanes of the hinterland, with varied scenery and some fine views.

Starting from the Maes (town square), go down to the harbour between the castle and the statue of Lloyd George and turn left just before the car park. In 100 yards (100 m) go straight ahead at the mini roundabout and continue for 0.75 mile (1.2 km) to the next roundabout, passing the terminus of the Welsh Highland Railway (1). At this roundabout take the third exit ⇨ Porthmadog (A487), and in 100 yards (100 m) at the bottom of the short hill turn right ⇨ Saron and immediately right again down Coed Helen road ⇨ caravan park and golf course. Follow this road for a mile (1.6 km) to where it drops steeply down to the harbour (2). Continuing, the (by now unfenced) road runs for 3 miles (4.8 km) along the very edge of the Strait – sometimes flooded at very high tides – with fine views across the water to Ynys Môn *(Anglesey)* and, initially, back to the castle and town walls.

After passing the golf club and small boatyard there is an interesting little church in a field on the left (3), and then the southern entrance to the Strait comes into view, with Trwyn Abermenai on the Ynys Môn side and Fort Belan on the mainland (4). A little further on there is a rather exposed picnic site overlooking Y Foryd Fawr (5). In half a mile (800 m) the road takes a sharp left turn inland. In 0.75 mile (1.2 km) turn right at the T-junction to continue a further 0.5 mile (800 m) to the far end of the small housing estate of Saron and turn right at the X-roads ⇨ sign of a bird. This road takes us back to the upper reaches of Y Foryd Fawr.

Just after the bird watchers' hide on the right, the road turns inland again, and in 0.5 mile (800m) turn right at the T-junction. Follow this road for 1.25 miles (2 km) into the village of Llandwrog (6). In the centre of the village turn right ⇨ Dinas Dinlle and again right in 0.5 mile (800 m) at the T-junction.

In 0.75 mile (1.2 km) is the tiny resort of Dinas Dinlle (7). Continue along the sea front to Caernarfon airport (8) and, since the road ahead is a dead end, turn about and retrace steps to Dinas and follow the road for 1.5 miles (2.4 km) (ignoring the turn-off to Llandwrog).

At the T-junction turn right on to the A499; the high wall in front marks the boundary of the Glynllifon estate (9). Keep to this road for 2.75 miles (4.4 km) passing through the hamlets of Pontllyfni, Clynnog-fawr (10) and Gyrn Goch (we are now entering the granite region as opposed to slate), and turn right ⇨ Trefor. At the bottom of this straight road, turn right by the bus shelter and right again ⇨ y Traeth (the beach). There is a car park here overlooking the tiny harbour of Trefor (11).

Returning from the beach turn right into the actual village of

Trefor, and at the X-roads in the centre go straight ahead. As the street drops down slightly notice the attractive workers' cottages on either side.

On ascending, by the grass triangle turn left ⇨ Cwm Pottery. This narrow road climbs steeply, then takes a sharp left turn downhill to the pottery, before climbing again to the mobile phone mast on the left. There are fine views back over the narrow coastal plain and across Caernarfon bay to Ynys Môn.

Continue along this narrow road, with passing places, to the village of Llanaelhaearn (12) and turn right on the main road. The road now climbs steeply, with Yr Eifl (sometimes incorrectly called *'the rivals'*, it actually means *'two groins'*) on the right, and views over the peninsula to Bae Ceredigion on the left, to the little village of Llithfaen (13). Carry on straight through the village and in just over 2 miles (3.2 km) look out for a turning on the right (just after a big lay-by on the left) with signs to Pistyll Caravan Park and St Beuno's church (14). The road carries on through the hamlet of Pistyll before dropping down – with fine views of the twin bays of Porth Nefyn and Porth Dinllaen – into the town of Nefyn (15). There are car parks down the first exit at the mini roundabout and about 0.25 mile (400 m) down the main B4417, i.e. the third exit.

Return journey
From the centre of the town go down Stryd y Plas (*Palace Street*), which, after a short distance bears left and rises steeply to Mynydd Nefyn. At the top of the hill there are views back over the twin bays, and Bae Ceredigion comes into sight. Passing through the hamlet of Mynydd Nefyn – a chapel and half a dozen cottages! – keep straight ahead with views of Yr Eifl to the left, Cader Idris to the right, and the mountains of Snowdonia in front. On reaching the T-junction bear right and shortly left at the major road. Continue

for 3.5 miles (5 km) to the village of Y Ffôr. At the staggered X-roads turn left onto the A499 heading towards Caernarfon. In 0.25 mile (400 m) turn right by a farm ⇨ Pencaenewydd.

From here on we are in a labyrinth of country lanes where it is easy to get lost – a map could well come in handy, but bear in mind that we are heading ultimately for Caernarfon. In 0.75 mile (1.2 km) after a wooded valley and where the road bears sharply right, keep left by the post box again ⇨ Pencaenewydd. In 0.5 miles (800 m) go straight ahead at the X-roads. The tall TV mast at Nebo comes into view and this is roughly the direction in which to head.

In 3 miles (4.8 km) look out for a cottage with the name Efail Pensarn written on a white stone, and where the road bends to the right, but keep to the left of this cottage. Carry on along this narrow road with views to the right over the valley to the foothills of Snowdonia, for 2.5 miles (4 km) to a stubby telephone mast. Shortly after, turn right downhill, ignoring the lane coming in from the right at the left-hand bend. At the next T-junction turn right and almost immediately left ⇨ Pontllyfni and Tai'n Lôn. Again, distant views to Mynydd Caergybi (*Holyhead mountain*).

Passing through the neat hamlet of Tai'n Lôn, turn right at the next T-junction ⇨ Llanllyfni. Follow this road for just over 2 miles (3.2 km) passing alongside a stream and under a disused railway bridge, then under a new bridge to arrive in the village of Llanllyfni (16). Turn left on the main road and continue down the main street. At the new roundabout on the approaches to Penygroes turn left and then right onto the new by-pass. Straight ahead at the next roundabout by the Inigo Jones slate works on the left (which is open to visitors). Bear right at the next roundabout and ahead at the next into the hamlet of Dinas (17) to drop down into Bontnewydd. Go ahead at the roundabout in the village then take the first exit at the next to get back to Caernarfon Castle from where we started.

1. The *Welsh Highland Railway* was built to run from Porthmadog through the heart of Snowdonia to join what was then the main line at Dinas, just south of Caernarfon. Opened in 1923; closed in 1933; reopened in 1934; finally closed in 1937; being restored since 1980 by Ffestiniog Railway. Using the trackbed of the old main line, it was rebuilt firstly to Dinas and is now restored from there as far as Rhyd-ddu as a tourist attraction.

2. Probably the finest view of Edward I's magnificent castle, built between 1283 and 1323 at the mouth of the river Seiont to impress and subdue the Welsh people. The several polygonal towers with banded masonry are unusual and thought to have been copied from Constantinople (Istanbul) by Edward on his return from the Crusades. It has been the scene of the investiture of the Princes of Wales since Edward II was born there in 1284, the latest being Prince Charles in 1969. The castle houses the Regimental Museum of the Royal Welsh Fusiliers.

A hundred or more years ago, Cei Llechi ('*the slate quay*'), where cars now park, would have been covered with slates, the products of the vast quarries of the Nantlle area of Snowdonia, and the harbour crowded with sailing ships waiting to load for industrial Britain, the Continent and the Americas. Those bound for the latter destination would also have offered passage, albeit an uncomfortable one, for emigrants to the New World. On their return they would bring back salt fish from Newfoundland, cotton from America and guano from Chile, having rounded Cape Horn. Some, indeed, may have been engaged on the lucrative but infamous triangular run – manufactured goods from Liverpool to Africa; slaves to the West Indies and America; and sugar and cotton back to Liverpool. Many of these ships would have been built, owned and crewed by men from this area – over 200 being built here in Caernarfon.

For a detailed heritage, full-colour guide to this historic town see **Welcome to Caernarfon** (available in five languages; www.carreg-gwalch.com).

3. No longer in use, Llanfaglan church is reached by a footpath across the field. The lintel on the north door bears a fifth/sixth-century Latin inscription.

4. Fort Belan was built by the first Lord Newborough at the end of the eighteenth century at his own expense to guard the southern entrance to the Menai Strait from the French. Although garrisoned by 400 men, they were never called upon to fire a shot in anger. The fort and associated dry dock are no longer open to the public, but when they were, Lord Newborough sometimes fired the cannons for the amusement of his visitors. On one occasion a projectile went through the sail of a passing yacht, landing on the beach on the other side near some holidaymakers. A tribute to accuracy, but frowned on by the authorities, and the good Lord ended up in court.

5. This bay, Y Foryd Fawr, dries out at low tide and is a favourite with bird watchers. Caernarfon airport is across the bay, formerly known as RAF Llandwrog. To the south are the distinctive three peaks of Yr Eifl. These peaks will dominate the skyline in the miles ahead.

6. Llandwrog was built to house the Glynllifon estate workers. The Harp Inn bears an 'Ode to Beer' on a plaque outside. The tall steeple of the church acted as a landmark for sailors entering the Strait. The interior, if open, is of interest; the west window is half concealed behind the organ loft and the side windows partly covered by ornate choir stalls. There is a row of attractive almshouses and a village well.

7. The 1.5 mile (2.4 km) of 'Blue Flag' sand at Dinas Dinlle is backed by shingle. It is a popular beach and there are a shop, café and toilets. The hill at the south end of the beach is of interest in that it was first fortified in the Iron Age, then by the Roman legions in the third century (from where it was within signalling distance of the main fort at Caernarfon), and in the twentieth century by the British – as witness the concrete gun emplacement at its base. From the top, the mountains of Snowdonia can be seen, with Yr Wyddfa (*Snowdon*) itself being the right-hand one of the two main peaks; at times the smoke of the little train ascending the mountain can be seen.

Legend has it that Caerarianrhod, a Celtic fort, was inundated at the northern end of the beach and that at very low tide stone remains can be seen. The northern coast of Wales has experienced hundreds of shipwrecks over the years (not always accidental!), particularly when Liverpool became the major port of embarkation for the Americas. Dinas Dinlle had its share of wrecks of ships that were trying to cross the notorious bar at the entrance to the Strait. One of the most bizarre occurred in 1971 when an ex-wartime amphibious vehicle was finally wrecked after the third attempt to sail to Australia! Another wreck was that of a Spanish galleon from which the locals collected gold coins for some years to come.

8. Caernarfon airport was built in 1941 as RAF Llandwrog, from where air gunners and navigators were trained. Alarmed by the number of accidents in the mountains, the then medical officer formed a special unit to seek and rescue aircrew. This became the first RAF Mountain Rescue Unit, which was to be copied in the UK and overseas. Whilst their primary duty is to Air Force personnel, they provide valuable assistance to all in need in the mountains and at sea. To this day the work is still carried on by helicopters from RAF Valley, across the bay on Ynys Môn. The RAF abandoned the airfield in 1945 and for many years it remained derelict. Nowadays it is used for private flying and pleasure flights. There is a small museum, gift shop, coffee bar and a restaurant in the old control tower.

9. The entrance to Glynllifon country park is just 100 yards (100 m) or so up to the left. The 70 acres (30 hectares) of this former home of the Newborough family is worth a visit. It is a SSSI (Site of Special Scientific Interest) with a variety of wildlife (including a colony of Lesser Horse Shoe bats). The estate workshops have been rebuilt, and the steam engine restored by Fred Dibnah. The grounds contain some interesting follies (including Fort Williamsbourgh, built in the late 1700s for military manoeuvres), and contemporary sculptures. There is also a memorial to the many quarry workers killed in the course of their work. Craft workshops and café are open to the public.

10. Clynnog-fawr church, dedicated to St Beuno, is well worth a visit. Its importance on the pilgrim route to Ynys Enlli *(Bardsey Island)* is shown by its size. Founded in the seventh century, the present church was built in the fifteenth/sixteenth century, and the saint is reputed to be buried in the little chapel connected to the main church by a barrel-vaulted passageway. To be seen: early stone sundial, massive dugout chest to hold contributions from the pilgrims and a pair of old dog tongs for removing unruly dogs from the church. Half a mile down the lane on the south side and across a field, is a good example of a Neolithic burial chamber, whilst 300 yards (300 m) down the main road, set back on the left side, is St Beuno's well, reputed to have healing powers. The village has a shop, hotels and toilets.

11. Trefor is dominated by the quarry, its *raison d'etre*. Whereas the slate quarries of Snowdonia roofed industrial Britain and beyond, so the granite of Llŷn paved the streets and roads. Quarries such as this produced *setts* (cubic blocks) for the streets of the towns and chippings for the tarmacadam roads. This purpose-built village was named by Samuel Holland after his foreman, Trefor Jones. The quarry opened in 1850 and closed in 1971. The stone was brought down from the various levels by incline to the pier, built in 1869 and extended with a wooden jetty in 1912. At one time there was a large reinforced concrete hopper on the pier, said to be the first such in Wales. Fortunately this eyesore was demolished in 1986. The harbour is now used by small fishing boats. The quarry's granite is of a particularly fine quality and, when polished, is in demand for architectural work, and for curling stones. There are shops, toilets and a hotel.

12. The main feature of Llanaelhaearn is the twelfth-century church, no doubt used by the pilgrims. Although restored in the nineteenth century, the old box pews and rood screen have been retained. The mountain up to the right is Tre'r Ceiri, with its superb example of an early Iron Age fort, a settlement of 150 huts surrounded by a massive stone wall. Those wishing to visit the remains of the fort will find several roadside parking places on the left just beyond the top of the hill out of the village (not the big lay-by on the right at the top) and access to the hillside across the road.

13. At the X-roads in the centre of Llithfaen, turning right will lead to Nant Gwrtheyrn, named as the valley of Gwrtheyrn (*Vortigern*) since legend has it that he fled here to escape his enemies, Hors and Hengist in 450 AD. Overlooking the sea in the steep valley is Porth y Nant, a former quarry village of some twenty-four houses,

23

shop and chapel built in 1863 to house the workers in the three quarries, the remains of which are clearly seen. Although the quarries closed in the 1930s the last inhabitants left in 1959 and the village became deserted and derelict until 1978, when it was restored and turned into a Language Centre for the teaching of Welsh. In its heyday, with the three quarries working and ships loading the granite at the three jetties, it must have been a vastly different place from today. As the only access to the village was down a rough, very steep track, supplies were brought in and shoppers taken out by ship, so that to some people Liverpool would be more familiar than, say, Pwllheli!

Another legend associated with the valley refers to three curses laid on the original inhabitants in time gone by that no son or daughter would marry another from the village; that there would never be any hallowed ground and the valley will live and die three times. They now await the third and final demise! There is now a good, steep and twisting, road down to the village and a café and visitor centre at the bottom. The area is a SSSI, being a fine example of exposed coastal woodland. It is also a good example of early twentieth-century quarrying, with remains of derelict buildings and machinery parts.

14. The tiny church at Pistyll was founded in the seventh century by St Beuno, who may have been laid to rest under the altar stone. The original wood and plaster building was replaced by a Celtic stone building and the thatched roof replaced 150 years ago. During restoration a fourteenth-century mural was found on the plaster of beef fat and lime. The font is Celtic, and water from a holy well nearby is still used for baptisms. Of the three windows one is for lepers. There is no electricity, and the church is lit by candles. The floor is strewn with rushes and herbs. Pilgrims passing through were accommodated in a hospice on the hill behind, and tenants of what is now Pistyll farm were obliged to provide sustenance to those who asked for it, in lieu of rent.

Among the many interesting headstones is that of Rupert Davies, the actor known for his portrayal of Maigret in the TV series of that name, who lived in the parish.

The large semi-derelict house overlooking the sea was built for Mr Goddard of silver polish fame.

15. Edward I held a tournament in Nefyn in 1284 to celebrate his invasion and occupation of Gwynedd, and the Black Prince granted the town a charter in 1355. In those days there was a large herring industry, and the town's insignia is three herrings. In 1747, 5,000 barrels of herrings were exported. Nefyn has for long played a leading role in the maritime history of northern Wales from the early days of building ships to the present-day sea captains. Over 100 ships were built on the beach at the far end of the bay, the last being the schooner Venus, 107 tons, in 1880. This activity required shipwrights, blacksmiths, sail-makers, rope-makers etc, and numerous taverns – fifteen at that time (now none) – for it was thirsty work. Since most of the ships would be owned and sailed by locals, this led to the teaching of navigation and the establishment of insurance companies (clubs). Shares would be offered in 64ths and many locals would have held those shares.

Buildings of interest include the old church with its sailing ship weathervane, and the old lookout tower alongside the new church. With a winter population of about 2,500 the town boasts three chapels and two churches. Nowadays the occupation of the townsfolk is looking after the numerous holidaymakers who arrive in the summer – the attraction being the magnificent safe beaches, superb golf course and the 'laid back' atmosphere. Clement Attlee, the Labour Prime Minister used to holiday here. There are the usual shops, bank, cafes and hotels. The rounded hilltop behind is Garn Boduan where there is a well-known Iron Age fort with remains of 170 round houses and a substantial curtain wall. The woods thereabouts were once owned by Ann Boleyn and Elizabeth I.

For a pleasant walk take the road opposite the school ⇨ Y Traeth (*the beach*), and then just before it drops steeply down, follow the path that goes round the wall of the castellated house on the left and out onto the cliff path. This path, with magnificent coastal views, looks down on the beach where, at one time, ships would unload their cargo directly onto horses and carts, and where now holidaymakers take advantage of the 1.5 miles (2.4 km) of glorious beach to swim and sail. Continuing on, the next bay, Porth Dinllaen (with its pub which is open in summer months and at weekends), can be seen, whilst down below is the tiny harbour where the few fishing and pleasure boats shelter behind a relatively new breakwater.

16. Llanllyfni and its larger neighbour Penygroes housed many of the workers in the numerous quarries in the Nantlle valley. It has few outstanding features, except Capel Ebenezer, which contains its original box pews, and the small church in the centre.

17. Dinas: the only claim to fame for this small community is in its residents both past and present. The former family home of the Armstrong Jones's – Princess Margaret's former husband's family – is now a hotel; Bryn Terfel, the opera singer, has been seen taking his children to the local school; Dafydd Wigley, leader of Plaid Cymru for many years, and a former MP, has a house here.

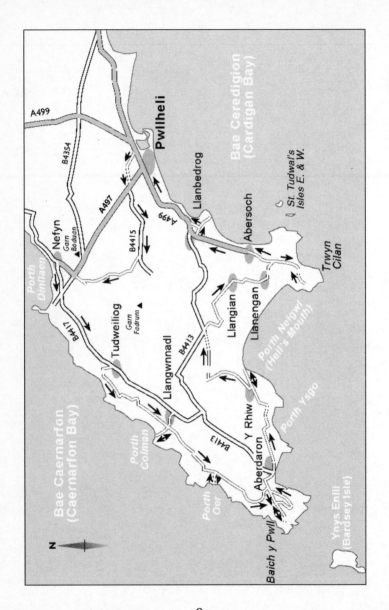

28

Link 2

Nefyn – Pwllheli – Nefyn

Distance: 54 miles (87 kilometers)
Time: 3 hours plus stops

Description
The Llŷn peninsula is not part of the Snowdonia National Park and is not strictly part of the remit of this book, but with 50 miles (80 km) of designated Heritage Coast, steeped in maritime and heritage history, it is obviously an area not to be overlooked. This route explores the coastline whilst at the same time following in the footsteps of the pilgrims who made their way to Ynys Enlli (*Bardsey island*) in their thousands.

From the centre of Nefyn take the A4417 ⇨ Aberdaron. In 1.25 miles (2 km) at the diagonal X-roads in Morfa Nefyn fork right ⇨ Golf and Porth Dinllaen. This straight road leads up to the golf club but halfway along at the X-roads, by a new block of flats, a right turn leads down to the beach with limited on-road parking. However, going straight ahead there is a National Trust car park in 100 yards (100 m) or so. Go to the far end of the park to get a fine view of the National Trust-owned tiny hamlet of Porth Dinllaen, nestling right down on the beach (1).

Returning to the X-roads, turn right by the block of flats and in 300 yards (300 m) turn right again, back onto the A4417. Dipping down into the village of Edern (2) carry on for another 3.75 miles (6 km) and turn right at the sign announcing the village of Tudweiliog. Follow this road round, ignoring any roads on the right, to Towyn farm on the left (3). Carry on to the next farm on the right and just after, where the road bends round to the left, take the road coming in on the right and then a sharp left (the rough road in front leads down to Porth Ysgaden [4]). Continue along the road, doing a dog-leg through the farm called Tyddyn, and ignoring farm roads coming in from the right and left, for a mile (1.6 km), until it drops down to a bridge over a stream with a car park on the right (5). At the next X-roads turn right and then, opposite the chapel, left ⇨ Porth Iago and Porthor. (If you wish to have a look at Porth Colmon [6] go ahead for 0.75 mile, 1.2 km.) Follow this road for 3 miles (4.8 km), ignoring side roads, and turn right by the semi-derelict farm and duck pond in front ⇨ Aberdaron and Uwchmynydd. Almost immediately the road on the right leads to Porth Iago, another popular small bay, but keep ahead for 0.75 mile (1.2 km) on this straight road. Part-way along, a lane on the right leads to Porthor (7) car park if you wish to visit this pretty National Trust bay. A little further on, just past the farm, there is a small National Trust picnic area, from where a short walk across the fields leads to a scenic cliff path overlooking the two offshore rock outcrops, Dinas Fawr and Dinas Bach. (It must be said that on the last visit the lane was very muddy and gated!)

Half a mile (800 m) further on, turn right in front of a cottage and follow this narrow and twisting lane, ignoring side roads, and turn right and right again at the staggered X-roads ⇨ Uwchmynydd. Follow this narrow road, ignoring side roads on the left, for just under 2 miles (3.2 km) to cross a cattle grid and out onto open land with the first views of Ynys Enlli. There are plenty of places to picnic off-road and for walks. Energetic people can climb up the hill to the former coastguard lookout (8), but the less energetic can drive up the concrete road to a parking space at the top.

Retrace the route back to the cattle grid, with views of Snowdonia as a backdrop and, at certain times of year, a wonderful display of purple heather and yellow gorse in the foreground. In 1.5 miles (2.4 km) opposite a row of white-washed cottages turn right down a narrow twisting lane, and at the next T-junction turn left and then left again by a farm. Half a mile (800 m) further on is the National Trust property, Cwrt, with a picnic area and track leading down to Porth Meudwy, from where many of the pilgrims set sail for Ynys Enlli.

Continue to the next T-junction and turn right and shortly right again ⇨ Aberdaron. From the top of the hill look down on this pretty village, and at the bottom turn right over the bridge into the centre (9).

Leave the village up the steep hill with the pretty little church and views over the bay on the right, and in 2 miles (3.2 km) take the minor road on the right at the X-roads by the phone box. In 0.5 mile (800 m) you will come to a deserted farm and duck pond. This is Ysgo (10).

Continuing the drive take a right U-turn just past the little church on the left and shortly rejoin the main road to turn right. At the top of the hill is the hamlet of Rhiw (11). Turn left to pass the PO and village hall and turn right at the next T-junction – don't be put off by the sign 'unsuitable for wide vehicles': it is a good road with wide views down to the vast expanse of Porth Neigwl (12). The road follows the shoulder of Mynydd Rhiw and, at its high point, there are remains of a Neolithic stone axe factory in a small parcel of National Trust land on the left – difficult, if not impossible, to find in amongst the gorse and heather!

There is a pleasant and easy walk from here up to the summit of the mountain with its radio masts, radar station and glorious views over the western end of the peninsula. Below the road on the right is a burial chamber, holy well and hut circles.

Continue for just over 2 miles (3.2 km) and turn right at the T-junction and right again at the next junction, at the edge of Botwnnog. Just over the bridge turn right ⇨ Llangïan. Look out for the interesting little church of Llandegwning with its unusual detached round tower set on a small octagonal tower, on the left.

Turn left at the next T-junction and then right at the next X-roads ⇨ Abersoch, Llangïan, Llanengan and Porth Neigwl, to enter the pretty little village of Llangïan (13). Follow the road through the village on to the next village of Llanengan (14) and turn left by the church and then almost immediately right up a narrow and steep lane. At the T-junction turn right ⇨ Bwlchtocyn, and in the next hamlet of Sarn Bach turn right again. Follow this road for some 1.5 miles (2.4 km) to Cilan headland (15), turning right by a bungalow to cross a cattle grid and onto common land where one can park. This road leads nowhere, so we must return back to Sarn Bach and then turn right in the direction of Abersoch (16). Entering the one-way system turn left as required and then right at the end of the street by the Harbour Hotel. At the main road go straight ahead into the centre of the village. There is a car park and access to the beach down the lane next to the petrol station; the tiny harbour is down to the left.

Going round the one-way system, this time turn left onto the A499 ⇨ Pwllheli over the bridge with a boatyard on the right. In 1.5 miles (2.4 km) look out for a narrow road on the right by a red post box and just before the riding stables. This narrow lane has a sharp right turn followed by a U-turn to the left with a lane coming in from the right (this, dead end, single track lane leads to a small car park with access to a fine sandy beach). At the top of the hill is a small parking area where the lane opposite leads up to Llanbedrog headland – Mynydd Tir y cwmwd, which is a good place for a walk with extensive views over Bae Ceredigion.

The road now drops steeply down to Llanbedrog (17). Turn to

the right at the bottom of the hill and follow round to the left to join the main A499 road by a petrol station. This is now a straight road of 4 miles (6.5 km) to Pwllheli (18). At the roundabout go ahead into the town. Just after the road bends to the right by the police station and just before the pedestrian crossing turn right down Cardiff Road and continue to the promenade. At the far end of the promenade follow the road round to the left and go along the Cob (embankment) to the mini roundabout by the station, turning left to the main roundabout in the town centre.

Return journey

Heading back to Nefyn, from the main roundabout take the street alongside the Mitre Hotel and then the second street on the left by the Whitehall Hotel. This road joins the main A497 road, where you should turn right into the village of Efailnewydd. Turn left in the village ⇨ Rhydyclafdy and after 3 miles (4.8 km) take the road on the right ⇨ Dinas. A mile (1.6 km) further on fork off to the right of the cottage directly in front, and a little further on take the road to the right ⇨ Nefyn by the grass triangle. Drop down into a wooded valley, and climbing up notice the plantation of eucalyptus trees on the left. Continue for a couple of miles (3.2 km) and then turn right at the T-junction. Straight ahead at the roundabout back into Nefyn.

For detailed, heritage, full-colour guides to this area, see **Welcome to Pwllheli, Welcome to Aberdaron/Nefyn**, and **Welcome to Llanbedrog/Abersoch**, (available in Welsh and English editions; www.carreg-gwalch.com).

1. The collection of cottages and one pub right on the beach, which comprises Porth Dinllaen, now owned by the National Trust, was once a thriving harbour. Over 70 ships were built here, the last being the *Annie Lloyd*, a 149 ton brigantine in 1876. It is recorded that in 1804, 700 vessels visited the harbour – 100 in one month. With this activity a harbour master was appointed, a position which the lifeboat coxswain holds to this day. The duties are no longer so arduous: it is a popular port of call for visiting yachtsmen, for whom no doubt the handy pub, the Tŷ Coch, is an attraction.

In the mid 1800s there was a proposal to make this tranquil spot the ferry terminal for Ireland. Fortunately this idea was defeated in parliament by one vote and Caergybi *(Holyhead)* won this dubious honour. The railway, which had been built as far as Pwllheli, was extended no further, and the building, called Whitehall, which was intended to be a hotel, was instead turned into holiday cottages.

· For many years smuggling was a major occupation with supplies coming in from Ireland, the Isle of Man and the continent; it is said that so much brandy was being brought in that the bottom dropped out of the market. The appointment of a customs officer and coastguards appeared to have little immediate effect.

A little further round, reached either by a path at the foot of the cliffs or by a rough road going up behind the Tŷ Coch, is the lifeboat station, established in 1864. Of the many rescues carried out over the years, that of *Cyprian* in 1881 is worth a mention; in this case the captain gave his lifebelt to a young stowaway and lost his own life as a consequence. Access to the hamlet is either along the beach at low tide, or across what must surely be one of the finest golf courses, for which a key is necessary. A very pleasant walk from the National Trust car park is along the beach, a drink at the Tŷ Coch, and return across the golf course. There is a lovely sheltered sandy cove by the lifeboat station, and many people carry on to the point to watch the seals. A climb up to the now disused coastguard lookout is rewarded with fine views up and down the coast.

2. A little cove downstream from Edern is where the telephone cable from Ireland terminated, no longer used, though sections of the old cable can still be seen at low tide.

3. There is a car park at Towyn farm, and a footpath across the field opposite leads to a lovely sandy bay.

4. Porth Ysgaden is a natural harbour where ships unloaded coal and limestone. It is now the haunt of divers searching for lobsters.

5. This beautiful, mile-wide beach is reached by crossing back over the bridge and taking the footpath on the left across a couple of fields. The beach, with rocky outcrops, is popular with those in the know.

6. Porth Colmon is home to two of three small fishing boats. Perhaps its main claim to fame was in 1901 when the *Stewart*, carrying a cargo of whisky, was wrecked hereabouts, no doubt to the enjoyment of the locals!

7. Porthor is also known as 'whistling sands' – so called because the sand screeches (rather than whistles) when walked on, due apparently to the rounded quartz crystals of the grains. This National Trust beach between rocky headlands is understandably popular with holidaymakers. There is a café – one of the few beaches to have one. On the hill just behind the car park, jasper (the semi-precious stone) was excavated in the eighteenth and nineteenth centuries.

8. This magnificent headland, Braich y Pwll (sometimes known as the 'Land's End of Wales') is now owned by the National Trust. From the now disused coastguard lookout, the views are spectacular, from Ynys Môn to the north, across the wide expanse of Bae Ceredigion to the Preseli hills in the south and in front, across the treacherous sound, Ynys Enlli (*Bardsey island*).

The island is roughly a mile (1.6 km) long by 0.5 mile (800 m), rising to a height of 547 feet (167 m). There were once six farms on the island but now only the custodian farms. The island is a bird and field observatory, noted for Manx Shearwaters. It is supervised by a warden. Trips can be arranged from Aberdaron. A monastery was founded by St Cadfan in the sixth century but the only remains to be seen today are those of the thirteenth-century Augustinian St Mary's Abbey, where 20,000 saints are said to be buried – along with Lord Newborough, whose family owned the island for many generations. Many monks fled here from Bangor Is-coed to avoid persecution, and it was considered that, because of the dangerous crossing, three visits to Ynys Enlli were the equivalent to one to Rome. The lighthouse, built in 1821, is now fully automated.

Bae Ceredigion is home to bottle-nose dolphins as well as porpoises; the odd small whale and leather-back turtles have been known to migrate here from the Caribbean.

During both wars the point was a defended lookout post, hence the concrete road and paths. A number of ships were sunk off the island in both wars, including six torpedoed in five days in 1917.

9. Aberdaron: this quaint village was the last port of call for the pilgrims, and they may well have partaken of a meal at the Gegin Fawr before starting on the last stage of their journey across the hazardous Bardsey Sound to Ynys Enlli. Today Gegin Fawr serves afternoon teas to holidaymakers. The church, whose graveyard has had to be protected from the encroaching sea, is dedicated to St Hywyn and dates back to the twelfth century. Inside are two inscribed burial stones from the sixth century. In the early 1800s, the church, being in a bad state of repair, was replaced by a new one on the outskirts of the village. This proved unpopular and the new building is now disused, and the congregation returned to the old church, newly restored, in 1868. A recent incumbent was the well-known poet and nationalist R. S. Thomas, but perhaps the village's most famous character was Dic Aberdaron (Richard Robert Jones) who in the late eighteenth century was a self-taught linguist – some say he could speak fifteen languages, others thirty-five! He compiled Welsh, Greek and Hebrew dictionaries which can be seen in St Asaph Cathedral where he is buried.

In 1405 the Tripartite Indenture was signed here whereby Wales would be independent under Owain Glyndŵr, northern England under the Percys, and the south under the Mortimers – a plan ruined by Henry IV.

10. For those who like a short walk a signposted footpath on the right by Ysgo farm buildings leads to the National Trust beach of Porth Ysgo. There are wooden steps down to the small sandy bay, but you can also follow the path round the hillside behind and up the next little valley, leading back onto the road and a short walk back to the car, passing an interesting little church – a walk of about a mile.

There are reminders of the area's industrial past: the mining of manganese – a mineral used in the manufacture of steel. The mines were worked from the mid-nineteenth century until 1946; 45,000 tons being produced during this period. Remains of this industry can be seen, but take care when exploring.

A pier was built at Porth Alwm (next to Ysgo) in 1902 at a cost of £182, together with an incline to take the ore down to the waiting ships. The pier has gone, but the line of the incline and associated buildings are still to be seen.

On a completely different note, 0.5 mile (800 m) to the west is

Porth Cadlan, where a recent study (with apparently ample evidence!) has suggested that this is the site of the last battle fought by King Arthur, and that after being wounded he was taken by boat to Ynys Enlli; but then Arthur has been said to have been connected with numerous other places in the UK!

11. The area around Rhiw abounds with archaeological remains; the craggy summit on the right was a hill fort, and there are hut circles and enclosures down its far slopes. There are further manganese mines on Mynydd Rhiw – the mountain behind the hamlet. During the Second World War 60,000 tons of ore were produced here, being taken by aerial ropeway to a pier at the foot of the hill.

Taking the road straight ahead rather than turning left leads steeply down to Plas yn Rhiw, a small sixteenth-century manor house and garden. Restored by the three Keating sisters in 1938, it was subsequently handed over to the National Trust.

12. Porth Neigwl, with its four mile (6.5 km) stretch of sand, looks inviting, but its English name, *Hell's Mouth*, suggests otherwise. Many a ship has come to grief on these shores. In 1898 the good ship *Twelve Apostles* was blown ashore, fortunately with no loss of life, which prompted the captain to send a message to Lloyds reading: '*Twelve Apostles* making water in Hells Mouth'.

Others were not so lucky; in 1629 a French vessel carrying wealthy members of the aristocracy, lured by false lights of the 'wreckers', hit the rocks, and it is said that the locals attacked the survivors with ferocity, killing many and even cutting off their fingers for their rings! Thereafter seafarers had a dread of being stranded on these shores. Apart from the wreckers on land there were pirate ships at sea in the seventeenth century and, surprisingly,

Arab traders who, in one raid on Caergybi (*Holyhead*) captured 100 persons for the white slave markets of north Africa!

During the Second World War there was an airfield on the flat hinterland behind the bay for gunnery and bombing training, the target being out in the bay.

13. Llangïan: in the churchyard of the simple thirteenth/fifteenth-century church there is a stone pillar bearing a Latin inscription stating that the remains of Melius the doctor, son of Martinus, lie here – thought to be fifth/sixth century.

14. Llanengan has a fine fifteenth-century pilgrims' church whose three bells are thought to have come from the abbey on Ynys Enlli. The church has an interesting interior with an offertory chest, an octagonal font and fine rood screen.

The village was the birthplace of Harold King in 1887 – prominent in the development of aspirin, anti-malaria drugs and steroids.

Lead was once mined on the hill behind the village, as witness the remaining buildings.

15. The views from Cilan headland overlooking Hell's Mouth are spectacular, as is the display of gorse and heather in the summer. A narrow gully path leads steeply down to Trwyn y Ffosle where, as the name suggests, there are fossils to be found. Further along to a prominent hillock on the cliff edge, Trwyn Carreg–y-tir, the very interesting rock strata of the cliffs can be seen, together with traces of mining activity.

16. Abersoch is extremely popular with the more wealthy set from Cheshire, and very many of the houses are second homes – thus the winter population of less than a thousand is ten times that number in the summer. The attractions are two fine sandy beaches, excellent sailing and a nine-hole golf course. One of the many beach huts was sold for £85,000 in July 2008! The bay is called St Tudwal's Road after a sixth-century saint of the Celtic church and, in contrast to Porth Neigwl, is considered a safe anchorage. In the past a number of sailing ships came to grief, but nowadays, for pleasure sailing it is ideal.

Of the two islands offshore, St Tudwal's East and West, the former has remains of a priory; the latter a lighthouse. At the far west end of the bay, lead mining was carried on from Roman times until the nineteenth century, the ore being loaded onto ships from a jetty at the now disused lifeboat station.

The village has all the amenities one would expect to find in a holiday resort.

17. Llanbedrog is another popular holiday spot, the long sandy beach being sheltered by the headland, the summit of which provides a panoramic view of Bae Ceredigion and the mountains of Snowdonia. A unique feature is the statue of a man looking out over the bay – the statue is made from salvaged metal.

Nestling at the foot of the headland is the Victorian Gothic manor of Plas Glyn-y-weddw, now a gallery and arts centre; there are extensive grounds and a licensed café.

The village, which is situated some distance from the beach, has shops, pubs, hotels and toilets.

18. Pwllheli is known as the capital of Llŷn. The town was granted a charter in 1355, and is the commercial centre of the area. A very popular market is held every Wednesday in Y Maes. Over 400 ships were built here up to 1880; the largest being 700 tons.

In 1936 three Welsh nationalists set fire to a building on the Penrhos airfield (some 2 miles west on the Abersoch road) in protest at the Westminster government military manoeuvres on heritage land here in Wales. This was probably the beginning of the present day nationalist movement, culminating in the establishment of the Welsh Assembly in 1999.

The airfield was attacked on five occasions in the last war, with the loss of two lives and considerable damage and the Maes was machine-gunned on one occasion.

Much earlier, in 1633, the town was terrorised by a pirate ship.

In Victorian times the town was developed as a tourist centre with the arrival, in 1867, of the Cambrian Coast Railway. This railway hugs the beautiful coastline as far as Machynlleth and then on to Birmingham. The line was intended to be extended to Porth Dinllaen when that place was being considered as a possible ferry terminal for Dublin, which never materialised, and the line went no further. One Solomon Andrews was responsible for much of the development of the town in the late Victorian period. The sand and shingle bank off shore was reclaimed, a promenade built and connected to the town by the Cob. A horse-drawn tram ran from the town out to the promenade and another along the sand dunes as far as Llanbedrog. The line closed in 1927 when part of it was washed away.

The beach, though extensive, is rather shingly, backed by dunes, but Glan-y-don at the other side of the harbour boasts beautiful sands. The harbour has been dredged and a marina built; this has proved very popular and is to be extended. It is now the leading sailing centre in the Irish Sea, hosting such events as the Celtic Regatta and other national and international gatherings. The Pwllheli lifeboat, founded in 1891, has rescued well over 250 people to date.

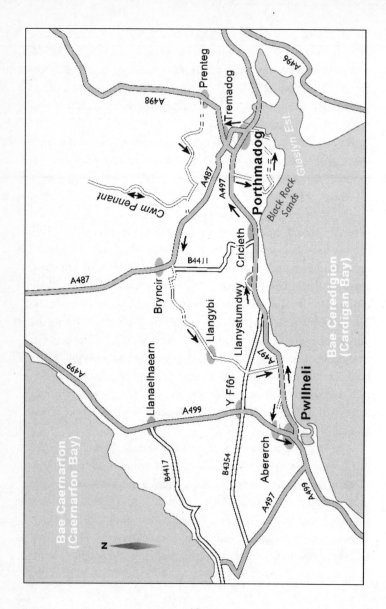

42

Link 3

Pwllheli – Porthmadog – Pwllheli

Distance: 45 miles (72.5 kilometers)
Time: 4½ hours plus stops

Description
This route follows the popular holiday coastline east to the busy town of Porthmadog, returning through the country lanes of the eastern part of the peninsula, including a visit to a saint's well and a medieval manor house.

From the centre of Pwllheli take the A497 ⇨ Porthmadog, but immediately turn right at the mini roundabout to pass the railway station, and then take the road on the left which runs between the station and the harbour. At the far end turn left over the level crossing and then right on the main road. Continue for 6.25 miles (10 km), passing Hafan y Môr holiday complex (1), and turn left ⇨ Llanystumdwy. Follow the road round, crossing the fine four-arched bridge into the village (2).

Passing through the village rejoin the main road. A mile (1.6 km) further on, at the start of Cricieth (3), turn right just after the 30 speed limit sign and continue to the first of Cricieth's two beaches. Along the promenade, passing by the castle, drop down to the second, more popular beach where there is ample paid parking. Just after the lifeboat house, at the bottom of the hill, turn left and follow the street up, over the level crossing to the centre of the village. Turn right back onto the main A497 road. At the top of the hill out of the village there is a lay-by on the right from where there is a fine view back to the castle.

Three miles (4.8 km) out of Cricieth, the road passes under a railway bridge with a rather nasty bend: IMMEDIATELY take the narrow, tree-lined road on the right (this turn could easily be missed so watch out!). Follow this country lane for 1.5 miles (2.4 km) to an interesting little church on the left, from where there are wide views across the Glaslyn estuary to Cader Idris and the Rhinogydd mountains.

Drop down and follow the road round to the T-junction. A right turn here brings you onto Black Rock Sands (4), where there is ample parking on the beach, but turn left and follow the road, through Morfa Bychan (5), and in 2.5 miles (4 km) near the brow of the hill take the road on the right ⇨ Borth-y-gest (6), and drop down to the small promenade, where there is parking at the far end. Returning - for this is a 'no through road' – and at the top of the hill, turn right to drop down into Porthmadog (7) onto the main street.

Return journey

Turning right here on the main street leads to the harbour and car parking, but turn left and go straight across the roundabout on the A487, passing Tesco, over the level crossing and on to Tremadog (8). In the village turn right on the A498 and in a couple of miles (3.2 km), in the hamlet of Pren-teg, turn left ⇨ Cwmystradllyn. Follow this very steep, wooded road, through a gate at the top of the hill, to come out onto open ground with fine views across the Glaslyn estuary. There are plenty of places to pull off the road for a picnic. Carry on beyond the little lake of Llyn Du as the road twists and turns until the T-junction (9), turn left, and right at the next junction. Just after Bryncir mill (10) fork right by a cottage to drop down to the river which at one time used to power the mill. At a sharp left hand bend there is an interesting tower folly in the fields up to the right, but carry on to cross the river, then turn left (11) and continue to the main road at Dolbenmaen.

Turn right along the A487 and in 1.5 miles (2.4 km) turn left on the B4411 ⇨ Cricieth. Shortly take the first right turn ⇨ Ynys, Llangybi and Llanarmon. (Getting into the maze of narrow lanes, it is easy to take a wrong turn and get lost, in which case make for Llangybi, Y Ffôr or even Pwllhelli.) Follow this road (ignoring the first road on the left which is incorrectly signed to Llangybi) and take the next road on the left ⇨ Llangybi for 4 miles (6.4 km) into the hamlet of that name (12), and in 0.25 mile (400 m) turn right ⇨ Llanarmon.

At the stop sign in the hamlet of Llanarmon turn right and immediately left to cross the major road ⇨ Penarth Fawr (13). Carry on to join the main A497 and turn right, continue for 1.25 miles (2 km). At the first roundabout take the third exit ⇨ Aber-erch (14), a little old village. At the end of the main street bear left and then right by the Ebenezer chapel. This leads up to the main A499 Caernarfon road, but turn left and follow downhill back into Pwllheli, crossing the mini-roundabout at the bottom and a sharp right turn, then straight ahead down Stryd Fawr (High Street). Turn left at the end, by the Whitehall hotel, to arrive back in the centre.

For detailed, heritage, full-colour guides to this area see **Welcome to Pwllheli**, **Welcome to Cricieth**, **Welcome to Porthmadog /Ffestiniog**, (available in Welsh and English editions; www.carreg-gwalch.com).

1. To the locals this will always be 'Butlins', one of the first holiday camps. In its heyday it could accommodate 17,000 people and had its own railway station. Many leading entertainers either appeared here or started their careers as a 'redcoat'. The advent of cheap holidays abroad took its toll, and though efforts were made to keep up with the times numbers dropped to the 7,000 mark, and so in the '90s the old original chalets were demolished to make way for a large caravan park. During the war the camp was taken over by the navy, as *HMS Glendower*, and many thousands of naval recruits, including the Duke of Edinburgh, will have 'fond' memories of their basic training here.

2. Llanystumdwy's claim to fame is Lloyd George, who although born in Manchester, lived most of his early life here with his uncle, the village shoemaker. He trained as a solicitor and was elected to Parliament in 1890 as member for Caernarfon, representing that constituency until just before his death in 1945. He became Prime Minister during the First World War. He lies buried on the banks of his beloved river Dwyfor just upstream from the bridge. His grave and memorial stone were designed by Clough Williams-Ellis, the architect of Portmeirion, who also designed Capel Moriah in the village. There is an excellent museum in the village, including the interior of the house where Lloyd George was brought up – the house of his uncle, the village cobbler.

Members of the Baptist church are still baptised in the river under the bridge.

There are cafes, shops, a pub serving good food, and toilets in the village.

3. Cricieth: this rather sedate family holiday and retirement town is dominated by its castle, built in the thirteenth century by Llywelyn Fawr (*the Great*). Seized and extended by Edward I in 1284, it fell to Owain Glyndŵr in 1404 and left to fall into disrepair. The view from the castle is breathtaking.

Beneath the castle, which has a small museum, is Cadwalader's renowned ice cream parlour.

There are plenty of car parks in the town, and the main street has a number of restaurants and small shops.

The town is proud of its floral displays and its biannual fair. There is an eighteen-hole golf course.

4. Black Rock Sands, this two-mile stretch of beach, from Graig Ddu *(Black Rock)*, at the western end to the caravan sites of Morfa Bychan in the east, is extremely popular with holidaymakers, since the tide recedes a long way and cars are allowed to park on the beach for a small charge. In 1907 the good ship *Owen Morris*, homeward bound from Labrador, was wrecked on Graig Ddu – so close to home!

5. Morfa Bychan consists almost entirely of modern bungalows, caravan sites and an eighteen-hole golf course.

6. Borth-y-gest: this quiet, semi-circular bay nestles beneath the mountain, Moel-y-gest, and, facing south, has excellent views across the estuaries of the rivers Glaslyn and Dwyryd to the Rhinogydd range of mountains beyond. There is a pleasant cliff walk from the car park at the far end of the promenade. The village was not always so sleepy, since at one time it boasted four shipbuilders' yards.

There are toilets by the car park and a shop and café nearby.

7. Porthmadog: the mile long Cob (causeway) was built in 1811 by William Madocks to reclaim 7,000 acres of land from the estuary of the river Glaslyn, at the same time establishing the town named after him. The harbour, opened in 1824, came into its own when the Ffestiniog railway came into town across the Cob. This 13.5 mile (21.7 km) long railway was built in 1836 and was originally horse-drawn, steam being introduced in 1863. It closed in the 1940s. Thanks to the dedicated hard work of volunteers it reopened as a tourist attraction in 1955. Some of the early locomotives and carriages are still in use today. The Welsh Highland Railway now links with the Ffestiniog, running the track along the main road for a short way before it enters the Ffestiniog railway station.

The vast quantities of slate produced by the big quarries of Blaenau Ffestiniog were exported worldwide from the harbour, and a considerable trade was built up with Germany following the great fire of Hamburg in 1842. In 1873, for instance, 100,000 tons of slate were shipped through the port. Many of these ships were locally built – more than 300 in Porthmadog alone. With the general decline in building sailing ships in the 1880s consequent on the arrival of the main line railways, Porthmadog was alone in continuing building ships well into the twentieth century, producing fine schooners such as Western Ocean Yachts, which were renowned the world over. Shipbuilding ceased in 1914.

The wide main street is always busy, and has a fair number of small shops, together with the usual banks and estate agents, three supermarkets and even a cinema.

8. Tremadog: there is more to this attractive little village than meets the eye. Developed by William Madocks in the early 1800s, it was part of his ambitious plan to make Porth Dinllaen the ferry terminal for Ireland – hence the London and Dublin street names. The attractive building facing the square was designed as a concert hall.

Lawrence of Arabia was born here in the house on the right as you enter the village – now a café and Christian Mountain Centre.

In the woods just outside the village on the Beddgelert road is Tan-yr-Allt, a fine Regency house Madocks built for himself. He rented it to the poet Percy Bysshe Shelley in 1812. Shelley was apparently wanted by the English secret police for writing

One of the main streets of the old walled town of Caernarfon

Glynllifon, the estate gateway between Caernarfon and Pwllheli

Clynnog Fawr by-pass

Nefyn from Garn Boduan

Aberdaron, the village at the western tip of Llŷn

A quiet corner near the old market hall, Pwllheli

Lloyd George Museum, Llanystumdwy

Cricieth castle and bay

Cnicht peak beyond the harbour bridge, Porthmadog

Portmeirion

Harlech castle

A long, empty Meirionnydd beach near Barmouth

Cadair Idris from the Corris road

Dyfi valley and Machynlleth

The parliament house in Machynlleth where Owain Glyndŵr held the first Welsh parliament in the fifteenth century

Aberglaslyn from the bridge

Tanygrisiau power station near Blaenau Ffestiniog

A heritage quarrying village at Llechwedd, Blaenau Ffestiniog

Welsh Highland Railway heritage train near Porthmadog

Dolwyddelan castle

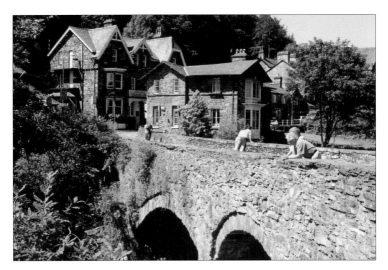

Pont-y-pair, Betws-y-coed

Tŷ Hyll, Betws-y-coed

The Bedol inn on the old drovers' road at Tal-y-bont, Dyffryn Conwy

Llanrwst bridge

Conwy castle

Llandudno from the Great Orme

'Gelert's' grave at Beddgelert

Llyn Ogwen and Y Garn

Penygwryd Hotel

Nant Ffrancon

Snowdon and Grib Goch from a lay-by above Nant Gwynant

Moel Siabod from the Crimea Pass

subversive literature in Ireland. After numerous travels through England and Wales he ended up at Tan-yr-Allt. The following year he claims to have been shot at by intruders and promptly departed. He was drowned in Italy in 1822.

Tremadog rocks are well known to climbers and most weekends they can be seen clinging to the rock face.

9. The road to the right leads up to rather bleak Cwmystradllyn. The lake supplies water for Llŷn. At the far end are extensive remains of a slate quarry, and on the slopes of Moel Hebog a street of derelict cottages. Also to be seen is the trackbed of the old quarry railway which ran down to Porthmadog.

10. Bryncir woollen mill, which has been weaving cloth for 150 years, was originally powered by a water wheel, which is still visible. Visitors can see, and buy, the Welsh tapestry cloth being woven.

11. The road to the right leads to beautiful Cwm Pennant, considered one of the most tranquil valleys in the area. The road meanders for 4 miles (6.5 km) following the infant river Dwyfor, to the substantial remains of a quarry at the head of the valley. The trackbed of the old railway joins up with that from Cwmystradllyn.

12. Llangybi church was restored in the late 1800s, but the chancel is fifteenth century and the nave probably earlier. A path leads down to Ffynnon Gybi – the well is ancient, but the buildings are believed to have been erected by William Price of Rhiwlas, the landowner, in 1750. The buildings consist of a tiny cottage for the keeper and an interesting toilet block! The well itself has two chambers of very clear water which is said to cure most ailments, particularly those to do with the eyes. Although roofless, the well is there for all to use. William Price also erected a row of almshouses in the hamlet.

13. Penarth Fawr: the medieval hallhouse, erected in 1460, has been well preserved and is well worth a short inspection.

14. Abererch: the mainly sixteenth-century church has some interesting choir stalls and a medieval dug out offertory chest. It stands opposite the prominent Ebenezer chapel.

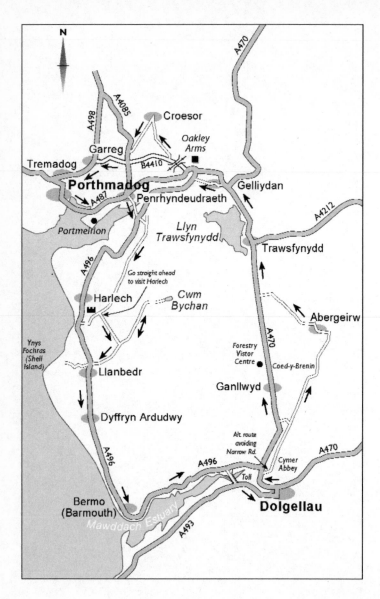

Link 4

Porthmadog – Dolgellau – Porthmadog

Distance: 76 miles (122 kilometers)
Time: 4½ hours plus stops

Description

This link takes in the wide sweep of Bae Ceredigion down to what is considered one of the most scenic estuaries in the country. After leaving the attractive old market town of Dolgellau on the return journey, the route passes through the extensive Coed-y-brenin forest, and open moorland followed by a foretaste of the actual mountains of Eryri.

From Porthmadog proceed down the High Street on the A487 ⇨ Dolgellau, past the terminus of the Ffestiniog Railway (1) and along the mile (1.6 km) long causeway shared with the narrow gauge railway (2). Turning inland, carry on for another mile (1.6 km) to the hamlet of Minffordd: the road on the right, just before the pedestrian crossing, leads to Portmeirion (3).

    The next village is Penrhyndeudraeth (4) passing the new timber and slate building on the right, just before the village, which is the headquarters of Parc Cenedlaethol Eryri (the Snowdonia National Park). Fork right, by the church ⇨ Harlech Toll (5). Having paid the modest toll (40p in 2008) cross the estuary on a bridge shared with the railway. At the staggered X-roads, on the main A496 road, go straight across up the narrow steep road in front. At the top of the hill by the phone box our route follows the road sharp right. (At this point there is a charming small lake, Llyn Tecwyn Isaf, ideal for a picnic, down the lane and across a cattle grid, to the left.) Ignoring

69

the road coming in on the right, our road drops down a steeply wooded valley to cross a stream and then rises to the Maes-y-neuadd Hotel on the left.

400 yards (350 m) further on, at the cluster of buildings that are Eisingrug, fork left ⇨ Llanfair keeping to the left of the cottage and derelict barn in front. In 0.5 mile (800 m) we come to the first of many gates, with a farm on the right. The lane now climbs to give panoramic views over Bae Ceredigion to Llŷn. Two more gates to the top of the very steep rise and the road opens out onto fields, and then a cattle grid. The single-track road on the left ⇨ Cwm Bychan is for intrepid drivers: there are seven gates, hairpin bends, and drops either side.

(This road, which is the chosen route, misses out Harlech (6), and those wishing to visit the village with its famous castle, or take the easier route, should carry straight on and then turn right at the next X-roads to drop down steeply into the village.)

Having negotiated the hazards of this lane you come to a wider wooded road with a good picnic site opposite, on the banks of the river Artro (6). Turn right to follow alongside the river for 2.5 miles (3 km) where a road leads off to the left over a bridge and left again (8), but carry on a little further to enter the village of Llanbedr (9). Turn left and follow the main A496 for 7.5 miles (12 km) to Abermaw *(Barmouth)*, passing through the villages of Dyffryn Ardudwy and Tal-y-bont (10). There are a number of large caravan sites taking advantage of the marvellous eight-mile stretch of sand along this coast: fortunately they are mainly below the road and thus not too obtrusive.

Entering the town turn right ⇨ Traeth, just before the pedestrian crossing, and follow the street over the level crossing and out onto the promenade where there is ample parking (11). Turn left and follow the promenade round to the little harbour and back on the main road turning right.

Follow the road alongside the beautiful Mawddach estuary, across which rises the bulk of Cader Idris, passing through the hamlet of Bontddu (12). Six miles (9.6 km) after leaving Abermaw turn right onto a private road ⇨ Tywyn by Toll (60p). This wooden bridge crosses the river Mawddach and the old railway line from Abermaw to Wrexham and on to Chester. The old signal box has been adapted for the use of bird watchers. There is a pleasant level walk along the track bed of the old railway following the estuary. Turn left on the main road ⇨ Dolgellau, and in a mile, just before the road crosses the by-pass, turn right on a secondary road ⇨ Dolgellau, to enter the town in the market square (13).

Return journey
Leave Dolgellau heading north over the bridge over the river Wnion to turn left ⇨ Tywyn and Abermaw and then, shortly, right onto the new road. Ignore the turn-off to Tywyn and in 0.75 mile (1.2 km) take the minor road on the right ⇨ Cymer Abbey (14). In 300 yards (300 m) keep to the right (the road ahead leads to the Abbey and is a cul-de-sac) and shortly after, fork left down towards the river Mawddach, which the lane follows for some 2.25 miles (3.6 km). High up on the right is the well-known Precipice Walk, much of which was originally made by sheep traversing the mountain side. As the name implies, it is thus very narrow and precipitous and unsuitable for those suffering from vertigo! The walk can be reached from a car park just up the next road on the right and is well worth the modest effort. There are remains of gold mines in this area.

After the cattle grid turn right at the T-junction and then sharp left at the X-roads ⇨ Abergeirw. The road now follows the river Gain through the beautiful Coed-y-brenin forest (15) for just over

2 miles (3.2 km). Crossing the river bridge turn right by the phone box ⇨ Trawsfynydd and Abergeirw.

The road now climbs leaving the forest for more open ground on the right. In a couple of miles cross Pont Aber Geirw, over the river Mawddach, and climb steeply over a cattle grid, the first of eight on this stretch, to come out onto open heath. Keep left where the road comes in from the right and drop down to yet another bridge, this time over the river Gain, to climb steeply, with a small copse on the left. Bear left after the next cattle grid, and then left again to drop down to Bronaber holiday village – a collection of chalets on the site of what was an old army training camp, with hotel and artificial ski slope.

The Romans have left their mark in this area and, just before dropping down to Bronaber, our route crosses Sarn Helen, their main road running from their fort at Tomen y Mur, just north of Trawsfynydd, south to Dolgellau to meet up with their road from Bala.

Turning right on the main A470 road, take the second road on the left ⇨ Trawsfynydd, into the village (16). Continue through the village to rejoin the main road and turn left. Just after passing the nuclear power station turn left ⇨ Gellilydan and on entry keep right following the road till it drops steeply down through woods to join the A496 and turn right into the hamlet of Maentwrog (17) in the beautiful vale of Ffestiniog.

Rejoin the main A487 and turn left. Rising slightly after crossing the river Dwyryd turn right at the bus shelter by the Oakley Arms (18) ⇨ Rhyd. Shortly the lovely Llyn Mair comes into sight. There are parking places on the right and a picnic site by the lake. There is a relatively short nature trail in the woods behind and a path round the lake.

Shortly after, pass under the bridge carrying the Ffestiniog railway line at Tan-y-bwlch station. Immediately take the narrow road on the right (unsignposted). This lovely road is well worth the effort of opening gates and perhaps having to reverse to a passing place. The road climbs through the forest and shortly after a cattle grid, comes out on top with glorious views of the Snowdon range in front and Moel Hebog and Moel-ddu away to the left.

Through the next gate and a short, sharp rise to open land. There are good views behind and to the left and a parking place for those energetic enough to want to climb either Moelwyn Bach or Moelwyn Mawr – both well over 2,000 feet (600 m) but the views from the summits are superb! Another gate and the road enters the forest again emerging to the full panorama of Snowdon. The distinctive pointed top of Cnicht, another 2,000 footer (600 m), comes into view. The road now drops down steeply to yet another gate and a bridge over a rushing mountain stream.

A further steep drop leads down through one final gate to the hamlet of Croesor (19). At the X-roads, approaching the houses, turn left where the road then drops down to run alongside the river Croesor. Two miles (3.2km) further on down this narrow attractive road is Plas Brondanw (20). Next, join the main road by the gatehouse and turn left ⇨ Penrhyndeudraeth. At the X-roads in the next hamlet, Garreg, turn right ⇨ Pren-teg and Tremadog B4410. Cross the beautiful river Glaslyn and then turn left ⇨ Porthmadog 3 miles (4.8 km). In 2 miles enter Tremadog and turn left for the final mile (1.6 km) to Porthmadog, encountering the new Welsh Highland Railway on the way.

For detailed heritage, full-colour guides to this area see **Welcome to Porthmadog/Ffestiniog** and **Welcome to Harlech/Bermo**, (available in Welsh and English editions; www.carreg-gwalch.com).

1. Ffestiniog Railway: one of Wales' leading tourist attractions, this narrow gauge railway, built in 1836 to carry slate down from Blaenau Ffestiniog, now carries tourists the 13.5 miles (22 km) up the beautiful vale of Ffestiniog to Blaenau where, if desired, one can journey up to Llandudno by the standard gauge line from a station built jointly with British Rail. Of interest to steam enthusiasts are the original engines, notably the unusual double-headed *Fairlie*. There is a shop and café at the station and refreshments can be obtained on the trains.

2. Porthmadog: there are spectacular views from the Cob towards the mountains of Snowdonia. At the end of the causeway is Boston Lodge, the engineering workshops for the railway, named after the constituency represented by William Madocks who built the Cob.

On the hillside above, hidden from view, is an eighteenth-century mansion built for Samuel Holland the slate baron. In the 1960s Bertrand Russell, the philosopher, lived there.

3. Portmeirion: this fascinating, fantasy village, in a magnificent location overlooking the estuary of the river Dwyryd, was conceived by the architect Clough Williams-Ellis in the 1930s. He collected buildings from all over Britain and abroad, assembling them after the style of Portofino. One can walk around, in and out, of this collection of odd but beautiful buildings, placed with the architect's eye for the most dramatic effect – the result is a bit like an opera set. There is a hotel where many well-known people came to stay between the wars, appreciating the privacy and discretion. Noel Coward wrote *Blithe Spirit* here, and in the 1960s the village was the setting for the cult television series 'The Prisoner', whose appreciation society meets here annually. Examples of what some might call the 'eccentricity' of Clough Williams Ellis are to be found in the area, particularly around his home, Plas Brondanw. There is no denying that he left an impression, and that Portmeirion is well worth a visit. There are extensive grounds to walk around, as well as the hotel, cafes, shops etc. There is ample parking with an admission charge.

4. Penrhyndeudraeth: the older part of the village is up on the hillside. The principal activity in the past was lead and copper mining in the wooded hills to the north east, quarrying and later, the manufacture of explosives. The main part of this village dates from more recent times, having been built in 1852 by David Williams of Deudraeth Castle, on what had been a stagnant pool surrounded by swamp.

5. At the bottom of the hill is one of the two stations Penrhyndeudraeth boasts (the other being on the Ffestiniog railway at the top of the village). A level crossing leads onto the saltings, the sea-washed turf of the estuary, spoilt unfortunately by the huge pylons striding across the estuary, but nevertheless a healthy place for a short walk.

On the approach to the bridge is the site of what was Cooke's explosive works dating from 1872, for the manufacture of gun cotton for use in the quarries. During the last war 600 people worked here. The plant, which had been taken over by ICI, was closed in 1997 and the site cleared to become a nature trail. The rickety-looking single-track toll bridge shares with the railway the crossing of the river Dwyryd.

6. Harlech's raison d'etre is its magnificent castle built, as others, by Edward I, at the end of the 13th century to contain the Welsh. It was impressively situated on a rocky outcrop which at that time was washed by the sea, and the castle was thought to be impregnable. However, in 1294 it was besieged by Madog ap Llywelyn and in 1404 taken by Owain Glyndŵr. A long siege during the Wars of the Roses prompted the song 'Men of Harlech' – so popular with Welsh choirs. Finally in 1647, this last Royalist outpost fell to the Parliamentarians. The castle is now recognised as a World Heritage site.

The sea has now retreated 0.5 mile (800 m), the intervening space being taken up by the Royal St David's championship golf course, beyond which there is a magnificent stretch of sand backed by dunes.

The far northern end of this beach is a National Nature Reserve and permission must be obtained to visit.

There are the usual selection of shops, cafes and hotels in the town. There is also a small theatre attached to the Further Education College.

To rejoin our original route take the A496 south and continue on this road to Llanbedr, passing on the way the Llanfair slate caverns to the left above the road. These are open to the public; some scenes of the film *First Knight*, starring Sean Connery were filmed on location here.

7. A pleasant diversion here is to turn left and follow the river Artro for 2.5 (4 km) to attractive Llyn Cwm Bychan. At the far end of the lake there is a car park and toilet. From here it is possible to take a walk up the Roman Steps to the pass in the Rhinogydd mountains. These steps, which have obviously been well laid, are certainly not Roman and were probably made in medieval times as a packhorse or drovers trail. Since the road goes no further, return to the picnic site.

8. This road leads up Cwm Nantcol, and if time permits a drive of 3 miles (4.8 km) to its end will not disappoint. First, just over the bridge on the left is Capel Salem, a typical old Welsh chapel, but what makes it different is that it was here that S. C. Vosper painted 'Salem', his very well known painting of a haughty Welsh woman in all her finery taking her pew in the chapel. The picture in the chapel is not, of course, the original – this hangs in the Lever art gallery in Port Sunlight. Copies were used to advertise 'Sunlight' soap. Many Welsh people will not have the picture in their house believing that an 'evil eye' had been painted into the folds of her dress. The key can be obtained from the caretaker's house adjoining the chapel.

A 2 mile (3.2 km) hill farm trail leads up from behind the chapel to Cefn-isa.

A mile up the road, is a picnic site and the start of Cwm Nantcol Nature Trail which follows the river with its rapids and waterfalls.

At the far end of the valley a farm, Maes-y-garnedd, is the birth place of one John Jones, brother-in-law of Oliver Cromwell, who was one of the judges signing Charles I's death warrant – whilst unknowingly signing his own come the Restoration!

9. Just over the bridge in this neat and tidy village, a road on the right leads past the ex RAF airfield, now operated privately, to Ynys Fochras (*Shell Island*) – an island only at high tide. This is an extensive but well spaced camping site and the attraction is the lengthy sandy beach, backed by sand dunes. As its name implies it is a great place for shell collectors.

The church is sixteenth century, restored in the late nineteenth century, containing a Bronze Age stone. Just south of the village is Maes Artro, a complex of model village, nature trail and craft workshops etc. with shop and restaurant.

10. Dyffryn Ardudwy: just off the road, on the left at the southern end of the village, are two good examples of neolithic burial chambers (signposted). There is another one, up the road on the left, towards Corsygedol, known as Coetan Arthur (*Arthur's quoit*).

In adjoining Tal-y-bont there is a car park and toilets by the river Ysgethin, also a museum of Old Country Life.

11. The 'modern' part of Barmouth was built on the narrow strip of land between a steep hillside and the sea when the railway came in the nineteenth century. The old cottages are perched on this hillside. The newer town basically consists of a main street, a railway line, and a wide promenade backing a long sandy beach.

The old, original church is just above the shoreline at Llanaber, a mile back up the road. It was built in the thirteenth century.

The present church, above the town, is unique in that it was built on Worcester sauce! Mrs Francis Perrin, widow of the son of the founder of the firm, was the principal benefactor. The foundation stone was laid by Princess Beatrice, Queen Victoria's daughter. During construction the tower collapsed extensively damaging the church and again Mrs Perrin came to the rescue.

In 1895, a Mrs F. Talbot gave the prominent hill, Dinas Oleu, above the town as the first property to be owned by the National Trust. One of her family, the Rev. Neville Talbot, together with the Rev. Tubby Clayton, later founded Toc H., the Christian fellowship in memory of Lt. Gilbert Talbot killed in action.

At the harbour end of the promenade is an unusual round lock-up built in 1820, to house drunken sailors and gold miners from further up the estuary; it is divided to separate the men from the women.

There is a Maritime and Lifeboat Museum. The lifeboat is kept busy and in 1965 they were called out to rescue the local boat

'Violet Sinclair' in June and August, and again the following year in March. Finally in June of that year the sailor was persuaded to give up sailing!

During the season a ferry operates across the estuary to the Fairbourne narrow gauge railway. The old harbour is just around the corner from where, in 1781, they exported £40,000-worth of flannel and £10,000-worth of hand knitted woollen socks!

There is a good selection of shops, restaurants and hotels on Stryd Fawr (*High Street*) and the usual holiday facilities on the promenade. A must is to take a walk across the 0.5 mile (800m) railway viaduct (small toll) for superb views of what is considered one of the most scenic estuaries in Wales.

12. On this stretch of road there are a number of gardens open to the public overlooking Cader Idris, across the estuary. Gold has been mined in the hills behind Bont-ddu since Roman times, and whilst there is still 'gold in them there hills', it is no longer economic to recover and all the mines are closed. Traditionally the Queen's wedding ring is made from Welsh gold. The main gold rush was in 1860, when large deposits were found at Clogau, just above Bont-ddu, and mining was at its peak between 1880 and 1914, when 8,000 lbs (3,600 kgs) were produced.

If walking in the hills behind here do not attempt to explore the many holes in the ground where people have been trying to find the elusive metal.

13. Dolgellau: set in the valley at the confluence of the rivers Wnion and Mawddach, this charming market town was the administrative capital of what was the county of Meirionnydd. The narrow twisting streets flanked by fine stone buildings are quite unique. Parking in the centre of the town is limited, but there is a large car park down by the river. The town is popular with walkers due to its close proximity to Cader Idris and within easy reach of other well-known walks. The church, though not particularly old, is worthy of a visit.

Dolgellau became a centre for the Society of Friends, or Quaker movement as it is more popularly known, in 1657 after a visit by George Fox the founder. Heavily persecuted, the adherents emigrated to join William Penn in Pennsylvania. Just south of the town is Bryn Mawr, the home of Rowland Ellis, who emigrated to America in 1686 adopting the same name for his new farm – a name subsequently taken for the famous American women's college. There is a Quaker exhibition above the Tourist Information Centre in Eldon Square.

There are of course all the usual facilities one would expect in a small town.

14. Cymer Abbey: established in 1199 by the Cistercians from Cwm Hir Abbey near Rhaeadr Gwy, it was never completed. All that now remains are parts of the nave with fine lancet windows. The setting on the banks of the Mawddach is fine, if one ignores the nearby caravan site!

[Alternative route: The next 13 miles (21 km) are on narrow twisting roads and for those who would prefer a more direct route, instead of turning right to the Abbey keep on the main road to cross the Mawddach by a new bridge, which hides the old prettier bridge on the right, and turn right in Llanelltyd keeping to the A470; there is a small church in a circular churchyard worthy of a visit. In just over 3 miles (5 km), following the scenic west bank of the Mawddach, is the hamlet of Ganllwyd with a car park and toilets on the right. From the car park a path leads down to the river tumbling over large boulders, whilst across the road, by the tin chapel, a steep rough road leads to Rhaeadr Du, a spectacular waterfall. The Dolmelynllyn Hall Hotel, now part of the National Trust estate, is a former home of William Madocks who built Porthmadog Cob. It has a restored Victorian garden. Two miles further on, on the left is the Coed-y-brenin Forestry centre with an exhibition of gold mining and recovery. Gold panning can sometimes be arranged. Many trails lead from here through the forest to the mines. There is parking, a picnic area, cafeteria and toilets. In just over 3 miles (4.8 km) in Bronaber, link up with the original route.]

15. Coed-y-brenin (*the king's forest*) so named to commemorate George V's Silver Jubilee, was established by the Forestry Commission in 1922. It covers an area of 21,000 acres (8,500 hectares) and there are 50 miles (80 km) of way-marked paths suitable for mountain bikes. There has been extensive mining for gold in the past and there is an interesting Visitor Centre at Maesgwm on the A470 road.

16. Trawsfynydd: this village overlooks Llyn Trawsfynydd, an artificial lake created in the 1920s to supply water for the Maentwrog hydro-electric station. At the north end of the lake is the first inland nuclear power station to be built in the UK which came on stream in 1965 and which reached the end of its useful life some years ago, but the process of decommissioning will go on for many years to come. The building, designed by Sir Basil Spence to fit in with the countryside, has a visitor centre and nature trail.

For the film *First Knight* a substantial mock castle was built on the lake, and many people from the area were taken on as extras.

The village is famous as the birthplace of the poet Hedd Wyn (Ellis Humphrey Evans), who was awarded the National Eisteddfod Chair for poetry in 1917, just a month after being killed at

Passchendaele. His monument stands in the centre of the village.

Also born here, in 1577, was St John Roberts, persecuted for being a Catholic during the reign of Henry VIII, hung, drawn and quartered at Tyburn in 1610 and canonised in 1970.

17. Maentwrog: the village takes its name from the large boulder in the churchyard, said to have been thrown there by a giant named Twrog but in fact is a residue of the glacier age!

Just to the west of the village is the hydro-electric station fed by waters from Llyn Trawsfynydd.

The village itself was built by William Oakley to house workers from his huge slate quarries in Blaenau Ffestiniog. He built Plas Tan y Bwlch, just across the vale of Ffestiniog, for himself.

18. The Oakley Arms: the pub is named after William Oakley, whose house is across the road: Plas Tan y Bwlch is now the Snowdonia National Park Study Centre holding short residential courses covering all aspects of activities in Snowdonia. The extensive grounds are open to the public. Oakley planted his initials in different trees in the woods across the vale above Maentwrog – he intended this to be an effort for posterity, but it is sadly no longer visible.

19. Croesor: what is now a tiny hamlet was once a thriving community – the quarries deep in Moelwyn Mawr up the valley providing work for many. Moses Kellow, the quarry owner, introduced hydro-electricity to his quarries at the end of the nineteenth century, making the community the first in the area to have electric light. He also invented a revolutionary rock drill. The track bed of the old railway that took the slates down to Porthmadog can still be seen.

Another son of the village was Bob Owen, a quarryman and a self-taught researcher and historian who became a noted literary figure.

The houses are dominated by Cnicht, 2,265 ft (689m) sometimes known as the 'Welsh Matterhorn' because of its sharp pointed profile when viewed from the south west. In 1958, the shoulder of this mountain was one of the settings for the film *Inn of the Sixth Happiness*, which starred Ingrid Bergman.

20. Plas Brondanw: this is the ancestral home of Clough Williams-Ellis (of Portmeirion fame). The gardens are open to the public for a fee, and well worth visiting to appreciate the architect's touch with the landscaping. There are numerous obvious examples of his work and sense of fun – some might say eccentricity – in the estate.

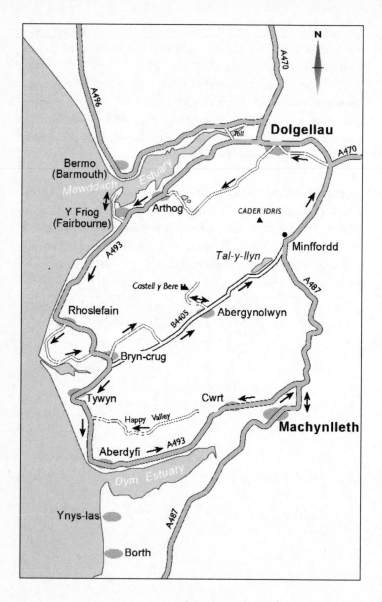

Link 5

Dolgellau – Machynlleth – Dolgellau

Distance: 76 miles (122 kilometers)
Time: 5 hours plus stops

Description

This drive is one of contrasts, taking in a high mountain, two beautiful estuaries, a couple of seaside resorts and an historical town. The driving is fairly straightforward, with only one stretch of 5 miles which could be considered a little difficult.

From the square take the street in the south-west corner by the market hall A493 ⇨ Tywyn. If you miss it, then you have to go round the town on the one-way system where the signposting is more informative. A third of a mile (1.5 km) after leaving the square look out for a narrower road on the left ⇨ Cader Idris, opposite a garage.

Leaving the built up area the road becomes pleasantly tree-lined before opening out into open country, with the mass of Cader Idris (1) coming into view on the left. At the fork in the road at Rhydwen farm keep to the right. Shortly afterwards, you come to Llyn Gwernan and hotel, from where one of the routes up Cader Idris, the Fox's Path, starts (not recommended).

A mile (1.6 km) further on at Tŷ-nant there is a lovely wooded car park with toilets. This is a free official park for the popular route up the mountain, the Pony Track. The view in front now is dominated by the sharp outline of Carnedd Lwyd, part of the Cader Idris range. After crossing a cattle grid the road becomes narrower,

85

and there could be difficulties in passing on this stretch – fortunately the steep drop is on the off-side!

After the next cattle grid take the road to the right ⇨ Cregennan Llynnau. This narrow gated road leads to an official car park (with toilets) overlooking these two attractive lakes with Cader Idris as a backdrop. This narrow, interesting road, rises steeply and then drops down even more steeply, but don't be distracted by the magnificent views ahead over the Mawddach estuary, towards Barmouth, for there are many sharp bends. Entering the woods of Arthog Hall, where there are footpaths to the scenic waterfalls, the road comes out on the main A493 with a very awkward left turn. Notice the row of colourful roadside cottages.

We now continue on this main road for 9 miles (14.5 km), passing through Friog (2 miles) (2). This cliff edge road has superb views across Bae Ceredigion to Llŷn and back towards Barmouth, but unfortunately, there is nowhere to park to admire this view until just before the village of Llwyngwril (3) where there is a lay-by on the right. There is another viewpoint just after the next village of Llangelynnin (4). Just over a mile (1.6 km) beyond this viewpoint, the road having turned inland, look out for a sign Rhoslefain and turn right ⇨ Tonfannau by the phone box. This avoids the main road and gives views out to sea and later over the river Dysynni estuary towards Tywyn. The army had a big camp here during both world wars.

Half a mile (1.8 km) after rounding a quarry, keep right at the T-junction and then follow the road down to rejoin the main A493 at Pont Dysynni to turn right. In the village of Bryncrug turn right ⇨ Tywyn for the straight run into that town (5).

Entering the town follow the one-way system to town centre and beach (don't follow the A493 which by-passes the interesting part). Carry on down the main street, at the end of which keep straight ahead under the railway bridge to come out on the promenade, where there is ample paid parking. At the end of the prom, follow the road round to the left and shortly, after the bridge over the railway, turn right on to the main road ⇨ Aberdyfi. Here is the start of the Tal-y-llyn narrow gauge railway.

Keeping to this road, in 4 miles (6.4 km) enter the town of Aberdyfi (6), having passed the popular golf course on the right. In high season, street parking in the town is well nigh impossible, but there is a large paid park on the right just after passing under the railway. The colourful Georgian town houses on the sea front bear witness to past prosperity and contrast with the lovely Dyfi estuary on which this prosperity was founded. Continue along the interesting front and out of town.

Look out for a small lay-by on the right with a footbridge over the railway onto what is known by some as Picnic Island, a small area of grass with seats and views across the estuary to Ynys-las Nature Reserve on the other side.

The road now follows the north bank of the estuary with some good views of the river. The next village we pass through is Pennal (7). Continue for a further 3 miles (4.8 km) to join the main A487 and turn right over the bridge ⇨ Machynlleth, shortly entering this historic town (8). There is limited parking on the main street to the left, but continue ahead and you will be directed to a large car park within walking distance of the main street.

Return journey

Head north out of the town by the way we entered, and over the bridge turn left on the A493 ⇨ Aberdyfi. A mile (1.6 km) after passing through Pennal, in the cluster of houses known as Cwrt, turn right ⇨ Happy Valley. Shortly after, this minor road becomes densely wooded, before opening out in a steep-sided valley after a couple of hairpin bends. Good views back over the estuary.

Three miles (4.8 km) after the start of this minor road there is an official car park on the left for those who want to walk up to Llyn Barfog (*bearded lake*) (9). This pleasant road, alternating between woodland and open country, eventually joins the main A493, and turn right in the direction of Tywyn. Follow the main road through the town, leaving as we came in on the long straight road to Bryncrug. Where the main road turns sharply left (Mace grocers in front) turn right ⇨ Tal-y-llyn and Craig yr Aderyn, and then immediately left ⇨ Craig yr Aderyn. This narrow, hazel-hedged lane has views to the left over the Dysynni valley and directly in front is the impressive high crag of Craig yr Aderyn (10).

Just after entering the woods, before getting to the rock, fork right ⇨ Abertrinant. The road climbs steeply through the woods, oak on the left, conifers on the right with mini-waterfalls alongside. Reaching the top the road drops down to the valley floor to join the major B4405. Turn left and after a right bend the Dôl-goch Falls Hotel is in front (11). Carry on to the next village, which is Abergynolwyn (12) turning left by the Railway Inn ⇨ Llanegryn. This is a short steep climb out of the village at the top of which there is a road on the right, to which we shall return shortly, but carry straight on, although having to return to this point, for there are several places of interest in the next couple of miles.

Turn right at the X-roads by the phone box and shortly come to the parking space for Castell y Bere (13). A quarter of a mile (400 m) further is the hamlet of Llanfihangel-y-pennant (14). There are toilets and parking here. Further up this road, in a cluster of farm buildings, is the ruined cottage, Ty'n-y-ddôl, former home of Mary Jones (15).

Return now, passing the Castell, turn left by the phone box, and at the top of the hill take the road on the left, mentioned earlier.

This road, high above the village of Abergynolwyn, has good views across the valley to Bryneglwys Quarry and the mountains of Foel Pandy, Mynydd Cedris and Graig Goch (the latter being 586 metres high). It then descends to the valley floor to rejoin the B4405, where it crosses the now infant river Dysynni. Turn left and shortly Llyn Mwyngil (Tal-y-llyn lake) comes into view by the Pen-y-Bont Inn and a tiny, unspoilt church on the right. Passing the popular Ty'n-y-Cornel Hotel, the road follows the bank of the lake with the foothills of Cader Idris sweeping down across the water. After several sharp bends the road joins the main A487 at the Minffordd Hotel (16) and turn left ⇨ Dolgellau. The road now climbs steadily up to the pass with magnificent views back from the lay-by on the left. Descending for a couple of miles to the main A470(T) at the abandoned Cross Foxes Inn, take a minor road on the left just before the 'Give Way' sign ⇨ Tabor. This road rises to give good views down to the river Wnion and the hills beyond before finally dropping down Dolgellau. Turn left on the main road and proceed back into the main square.

For detailed heritage, full-colour guides to this area see **Welcome to Machynlleth** and **Welcome to Aberdyfi/Tywyn**, (available in Welsh and English editions; www.carreg-gwalch.com).

1. At 2,927 ft (892 m) Cader Idris is the highest mountain south of the Snowdon range. The name translated is 'chair of Idris', but who Idris was is uncertain, though the chair is thought to be Llyn y Gader hemmed in by sheer high crags. The highest point of the mountain is Penygadair where, in Victorian times there was a refreshment hut, long since replaced by a rough stone shelter maintained by the National Park Authority.

There are four paths up to the summit. The Fox's Path, which starts from the Gwernan Lake Hotel, is considered to be dangerous and not advised. The Pony Path is probably the most popular and starts from the car park at Tŷ-nant, just a short distance from Gwernan lake; in days gone by this path was used by horses travelling from Dolgellau, over the shoulder of the mountain, to Llanfihangel-y-pennant and the Dysynni valley. The reverse of the Pony Path, starting from Llanfihangel-y-pennant, is the easiest route, but at five miles (8 km) the longest. Fourthly, the Minffordd Path, starting from the hotel of that name on the B4405 Dolgellau to Tywyn road, is the shortest but steepest route. Detailed guides for all these routes are available from National Park Information Centres.

2. The road on the right leads to Y Friog (*Fairbourne*), a not particularly attractive village consisting mainly of twentieth-century bungalows and chalets. What does make it attractive is the 15-inch gauge miniature railway, built originally as a horse-drawn tramway by Arthur McDougall the flour miller in 1895. The railway runs for two miles through the sand dunes to Penrhyn point from where, in season, a ferry crosses the Mawddach estuary to Abermaw (*Barmouth*). At the far end of the village opposite a phone box is a lay-by and lane leading up to the 'blue lake', a flooded quarry entirely surrounded by sheer rock faces. The blue colour is due to reflections from the slate walls and blue sky. There is nowhere to park up the lane so a visit to the lake has to be done on foot.

3. Llwyngwril: attractive small village astride the river Gwril. There is a Quaker burial ground above the village, and the remains of a Stone Age homestead.

4. Llangelynnin has an interesting little church down below the road, practically on the seashore, the interior of which has not been spoilt and the original pews and pulpit are still there. A horse bier, without wheels but with shafts at either end, once used to bring bodies down from remote places. There is the grave of Abram Wood, king of the Welsh gypsies.

5. Tywyn: this small Edwardian seaside resort was developed by John Corbett, a wealthy salt magnate from Droitwich after whom the main hotel is named - originally spelt with one 'T', but a second one was added when he bought the Corbet estate.

Notice the very ornate assembly rooms next to the late twelfth-century church. In the church is an early eighth-century stone which bears one of the two earliest Welsh language inscriptions – evidence in stone that Welsh is one of the oldest written languages in Europe. In the churchyard is a memorial to Ann Felix (see [6]) whose epitaph reads:

'Weep not for me my parents dear,
I am not dead but sleeping here.
Prepare, prepare to follow me
You cannot prepare too soon
For the night did come,
Before I thought it noon.'

The main attraction here, apart from the vast stretch of sand, is the world's first preserved railway, the Tal-y-llyn Railway, 2 ft (610 mm) gauge, built in 1865 to bring slate down from the Bryneglwys quarry to the main line Cambrian Coast Railway. There is an interesting Narrow Gauge Railway museum, café, shop and toilets, and ample parking close by.

In 1914 Marconi built a radio receiving station here, in conjunction with his transmitting station at Waunfawr (see Link 10 [16]). It is here that the first morse code message from America was received. The tall aerial masts have now been dismantled.

6. Aberdyfi's prosperity was founded on shipping – the export of slates, wool and oak bark for tanning – and the connection with the sea continues to this day. The Outward Bound centres were inaugurated here in the 1940s and they run a small Maritime Museum as well as sail training.

It is ironic that a tragedy, in 1839, should have happened in these supposedly safe waters: three young girls from Mrs Scott's Boarding School for Young Ladies, together with Ann Felix, the daughter of the landlord of the Britannia Inn, had accepted an invitation to supper aboard the brigantine *Favorite*. When Mrs Scott found the girls missing, a boat sent to the brig found it deserted, supper still on the table. The next day the ship's boat was found wrecked and the bodies of all scattered on the shore. Ann Felix is buried in Tywyn church (see [6]).

Interestingly, the railway passes through a tunnel under the town which has a station at either end.

At the far end of the promenade is a memorial garden to a small group of German-speaking immigrants who were trained here as commandos, and who rendered invaluable service during the Second World War. This garden is the start of a pleasant walk over the rocks to Picnic Island.

Another association with the town is the song 'The Bells of Aberdovey' written in 1785 for his opera 'Liberty Hall' by Charles Dibdin, one verse of which goes:

'Pretty maidens come again
Join us in a merry strain,
To all who live on land or main
Say the Bells of Aberdovey.'

The bells referred to are thought to have been rung from the legendary land of Cantre'r Gwaelod supposedly submerged off the coast many miles north.

Across the estuary is another popular holiday village, Borth.

7. Pennal: the Romans were here and built a fort on the banks of the river Dyfi at what was then the end of Sarn Helen, their road from the north, though it is difficult to find.

Although now an insignificant village, Owain Glyndŵr held court here in 1406 from where he wrote to King Charles VI of France setting out his vision and aspirations for Welsh independence, known as 'The Pennal Letter'. The original is in Paris, with a copy in the church.

During the realignment of the road some gravestones were re-sited to form a Heritage Garden.

The war memorial records the name of a VC of the First World War. There is also a memorial to six airmen killed when their Wellington bomber crashed in the vicinity.

8. Machynlleth: the most prominent feature of the pleasant market town is the tall clock tower, erected in 1878, by the town folk to commemorate the coming of age of Viscount Castlereagh, the son of the 5th Marquis of Londonderry.

Half-way along the wide main street is the building where in 1404, Owain Glyndŵr established the first and short-lived Welsh Parliament. Historical details are given in a small museum.

The medieval Royal House, near the town clock, has recently been renovated, and now houses the Tourist Information Centre. It is thought that Glyndŵr stayed at this house when in Machynlleth for the Parliament.

Not far from the clock is Plas Machynlleth, former home of the Marquis and given by him to the town in the 1930s. There is a shop, tea rooms, and pleasant gardens. The Plas is now being developed by local people as a community project.

The founder of the well-known Liverpool department store, Owen Owen, was born in the town.

9. Llyn Barfog: the origins of the name are uncertain; it may refer to the covering of water lilies; some say it is the shape of a face with the reeds on the chin as a beard, but whatever, on a nice day the 1.5 mile (2.4 km) fairly stiff climb up a rough farm track is rewarding. Half a mile south of the lake there is an upright stone known as Carn March Arthur (*hoof of Arthur's steed*).

10. Craig yr Aderyn: his prominent rock stands 762 feet (233m) high and dominates the valley. It is the only place in Britain where cormorants nest inland, and there are substantial numbers of choughs too. At one time the valley was flooded with the sea lapping its base.

11. Dôl-goch Falls: there is an official car park in front of the hotel for those wishing to visit these popular falls. The path alongside the hotel up to the first falls is easy; thereafter it becomes steeper with rough steps. To reach the top of the falls will take about 45 minutes, but the effort is well worthwhile. There are numerous smaller falls and rapids beside the path, which is well-maintained, as it climbs up through oak woods. This is a popular halt on the Tal-y-llyn Railway. Refreshments are available, as are toilets.

12. Abergynolwyn: this attractive village was once a thriving community when the vast Bryneglwys quarry was working. Now it is a sleepy little hamlet invaded in the season by tourists from the railway. There is a café in the new community centre.

13. Castell y Bere: this castle was built by Llywelyn Fawr (*the Great*) in 1221 and extended by his grandson, Llywelyn ap Gruffudd. It was the stronghold of these princes' power in southern Gwynedd. There is a short walk from the car park up to the castle ruins, from where it is easy to appreciate its strategic position perched high above the confluence of three valleys.

14. Llanfihangel-y-pennant: this little sixteenth-century church is worthy of a quick visit. It contains few relics except a medieval font, but it is a restful place, in this quiet valley away from the noise and bustle of the modern world.

15. This was the home of Mary Jones, the daughter of a poor weaver, who, in 1800, when only sixteen, walked barefoot the 28 miles (45 km) to Bala to obtain a Welsh-language bible from Thomas Charles the Methodist minister – only to find that he had none left. Inspired by her devotion he gave her his own copy so her arduous journey was not in vain. She kept it beside her until she died at the age of 88. This experience prompted Thomas Charles to mount a campaign which led to the formation of the British and Foreign Bible Society. There is a monument and a plaque to her memory.

This unmade road eventually peters out into the Pony Path, the longest but easiest path up Cader Idris.

16. In the hamlet of Tabor is a former Quaker Meeting House and graveyard. The Meeting House is now a chapel, but the graveyard warrants a visit. The Quakers formed a strong community in Dolgellau in the seventeenth century.

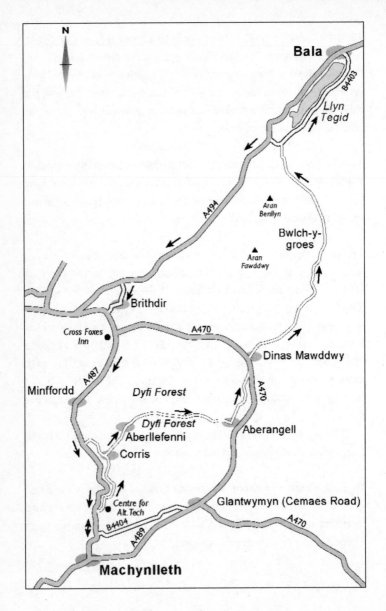

Link 6

Machynlleth – Bala – Machynlleth

Distance: 62 miles (100 kilometers)
Time: 4 hours plus stops

Description
This relatively easy drive follows the beautiful river Dyfi to its source, climbs to the highest road pass in Wales, then drops down to the largest natural lake, visiting a unique environmentally friendly site and an interesting church.

Starting from the centre of Machynlleth take the A487 north ⇨ Dolgellau and after crossing the river Dyfi, turn right following the A487. In 0.5 mile (800m) take the road on the right, the B4404 ⇨ Llanwrin. After dropping down to cross the river take the lane on the left and, in just over a mile, come to the Centre for Alternative Technology (1). Carry on along this lovely road, as it winds up the Dulas valley through the Dyfi forest, passing the hamlet of Ceinws, for a further 3 miles (4.8 km), then a sharp left bend and a bridge into the village of Abercorris (2). At the top of the street of attractive terraced cottages turn right ⇨ Aberllefenni. A mile (1.6 km) up this minor road is a Forestry Commission picnic site just below the road on the right. From here there is a way-marked 2 mile (3.2 km) forest trail. Carry on into Aberllefenni (3) and turn right ⇨ Aberangell. This lovely forest road climbs, with fine views, before, after 5 miles (8 km) dropping down to Aberangell (4) and turning left. Two noticeable points on this minor road are the neatness and colourful display of flowers in the houses, and the windfarm on the skyline. Keeping the river on the right, in a couple

97

of miles (3.2 km), ignore the road on the right ('weak bridge' sign), and passing an attractive cottage, with a river cascade behind, shortly join the main A470 by Meirion Mill (5) and turn left ⇨ Dolgellau.

Three hundred yards (300 m) up the main road branch off right, by the old filling station, to drop down to the village of Dinas Mawddwy (6). At the T-junction (toilets opposite) turn right by the Llew Coch (Red Lion) ⇨ Llanymawddwy and Bala. There is a grass parking area at the bottom of the hill with a footbridge over the infant river Dyfi with several paths leading off. Follow the road for 5 miles (8 km), ignoring roads on either side, to the hamlet of Llanymawddwy (7). A mile and a half (2.4 km) further on, a sharp right hand hairpin bend marks the start of the long steep climb up to Bwlch y Groes (8). Near the top ignore the road on the right which leads down to Llyn Efyrnwy (*Lake Vyrnwy*), the largest artificial lake in Wales and part of Birmingham's water supply. In the angle between the roads is a simple cross marking a place of rest and thanksgiving for pilgrims on their way to St David's in Pembrokeshire.

There is a car park at the top of the pass and a chance to rest before the equally steep descent. Over the cattle grid the first 1.75 miles (2.8 km) are steep and the drop on the near side necessitates great care. Another cattle grid marks the end of the very steep section and the start of the more gentle slope to the wooded valley floor. At the next T-junction turn right on the B4403 ⇨ Bala, following the edge of the lake (Llyn Tegid) (9). At Llangywer, half way along the lake, there is a good car park, picnic area, toilets and access, across the railway line onto the foreshore. At the end of the lake turn left to cross the outlet to the lake, the river Dyfrdwy, which will become the river Dee when it reaches the Cheshire border. On entering the town there is an official car park and toilets. In the main street of Bala (10) it is sometimes possible to find a parking place on the street.

Return journey

Continue down Stryd Fawr (*High Street*) on the A494 ⇨ Dolgellau. Although a good road, it has many bends and being one of the main trunk roads to Bae Ceredigion, tends to be busy, especially at holiday times. The road is not as fast as some drivers seem to think!

The Romans had a strong presence in the area, and this road follows the line of the Roman road from Chester *(Deva)* to join up with their north/south road, Sarn Helen, in the vicinity of Dolgellau.

At the head of the lake there are remains of a Roman fort, Caer Gai, built to protect this stretch of road, which now by-passes the village of Llanuwchllyn (11).

Just under 7 miles (11.3 km), after this village take the minor road on the left ⇨ Bryncoed Ifor (should this turning be missed, carry on to the next turning, the B4416, and join the other road in the village of Brithdir). Follow this minor road for 2.5 miles (4 km), the last mile of which, after the sharp right bend, is a straight run following, as it does, the old Roman road to Brithdir (12). Bear left onto the B4416. In just under a mile (1.6 km) through woods there is a very tight U-bend left onto the A470(T) so beware of fast moving traffic which is not easily seen. Turn right by what used to be the Cross Foxes Inn, onto the A487 ⇨ Machynlleth. This road rises to Bwlch Llyn Bach at just under 1,000 feet (300 m), where there is a viewpoint on the right at the top of the pass. There is now a long straight descent, with views of Tal-y-llyn lake, to Minffordd, the starting point for one of the paths up Cader Idris. Follow the main road round left to start the climb up to Corris Uchaf (13) and then down to Corris itself. In 4 miles (6.4 km) reach the bridge over the river Dyfi and turn left back to Machynlleth.

For a detailed heritage, full-colour guide to this area see **Welcome to Machynlleth**, (available in Welsh and English editions; www.carreg-gwalch.com).

1. The Centre for Alternative Technology: the CAT was started in 1973 by a group of likeminded individuals with the idea of being self-sufficient and environmentally friendly. Over the years it has grown, and many of its ideas are particularly important in the present climate. It is considered one of the leading eco-centres. They make use of wind, water and sun for all their needs. The site is much more than the disused quarry it once was and now provides one of the best tourist attractions for the whole family. There is parking, toilets and vegetarian restaurant. The centre also operates a café and health food shop in Machynlleth.

2. Corris: the narrow attractive streets were once the homes of those employed in the many quarries around, all of which have now closed. The unsightly spoil heaps are largely covered by the Dyfi Forest, which provides the main employment in the area. Enthusiasts have restored parts of the Corris Railway: this narrow gauge line was built in 1859 as a horse-drawn tramway and converted to steam in 1878, to serve the quarries up the valley taking the slates down to the river Dyfi. From 1883 passengers were carried, until the 1930s. It closed in 1958. There is a small museum, plus shop, refreshment room and toilets.

3. Aberllefenni: another tiny slate village surrounded by the Dyfi Forest. The slate has all gone, but the attraction is its situation. It is a good centre to explore the old quarries in the area (be careful, these places can be very dangerous) with many walks in the forest and some fine views. There is a Field Studies Centre.

4. Aberangell: the village has a superb situation overlooking the Dyfi valley towards Esgair Ddu 1,528 ft (464 m). Mainly dependent on the quarry above, the village finally arrived soon after 1868, when Sir Edmond Buckley, who owned the Hendre-ddu quarry in the forest, built a railway from Dinas Mawddwy to link up with the main line at Cemmaes Road. Primarily built to transport slate, it enabled villagers to visit places as far afield as Shrewsbury and Aberystwyth.

There is a thoughtfully placed seat at the far end of the village so that one can admire the view in comfort.

5. Meirion Mill, in the old railway goods yard, makes an interesting stopping place – plenty of parking, free admission, coffee shop etc.

Just a short walk from the car park is Pont Minllyn, an attractive twin-arched packhorse bridge dating from the early 1600s.

Maes-y-Camlan, situated half a mile before the mill, is where King Arthur is reputed to have fought one of his many last battles!

The region was once plagued by the infamous Gwylliaid Cochion (*red-headed brigands*) – killing and robbing the locals. They arrived in 1114 from Ireland and their name is thought to have been derived from either the colour of their hair or the amount of blood on their hands. Their reign of terror came to an end in 1554 when they were captured and put to death by Baron Owen on the orders of Mary I of England.

6. Dinas Mawddwy: this village is perhaps best described by George Borrow in his book *Wild Wales*. He came this way in 1854 and found it 'little more than a collection of filthy huts. But though a squalid place I found it anything but silent and deserted. Fierce looking red-haired banditti of old were staggering about and sounds of drunken revelry echoed from the huts.'

With the mines and quarries closed and the village by-passed it is now a very different place.

7. Llanymawddwy: in the churchyard of this pretty hamlet lies one of the two giants from this area, the other is alleged to have thrown a boulder from Aran Fawddwy across the valley to Ffridd Wenallt where it lies today with the indentures of his fingers! Soldiers are said to have sharpened their swords on the font prior to the battle of Bwlch y Groes.

The village lies on one of the old drovers' roads along which cattle and even geese, with their feet suitably tarred for the long walk, were driven to markets in England. A mile or so walk westwards is the waterfall Pistyll Gwyn, for those who like a gentle stroll.

8. At 1,790 ft (545 m) above sea level this is the highest road pass in Wales, and the views from the car park are spectacular; in front, you can see down Cwm Cynllwyd to the Arenig mountains. To the left are the two high peaks Aran Fawddwy and Aran Benllyn, both just under 3,000 ft (900 m). These two peaks seem to have had a fatal attraction for aircraft, there having been at least five crashes during the Second World War, killing eleven fliers.

Before the war Austin used to test their cars on this steep mountain pass.

9. Llyn Tegid (*Bala lake*) is the largest natural lake in Wales at 4 miles (6.4 km) long and nearly 0.75 mile (1.3 km) wide and is the source of the river Dee. It is extremely popular for all water activities, and fishing, for both of which permits are required. The lake is home to the rare gwyniad fish found nowhere else in Britain, and almost impossible to catch. Running down the south eastern shore from Bala to Llanuwchllyn is the narrow gauge Bala Lake Railway, using the trackbed of the old main line which used to run from the coast at Barmouth to Ruabon.

10. Bala is one of those towns which is always busy. The wide Stryd Fawr, where most of the shops and hotels are situated, is usually thronged with tourists, either passing through on their way to the coast or engaged on the many outdoor activities in the area. The town has a history of non-conformism as well as Welsh-language and culture. The impressive statue on the right at the beginning of the street is that of Thomas Ellis, liberal Chief Whip and local MP in the late nineteenth century.

On the A4212 out of Bala is the old Methodist College, now a youth centre, founded in 1837 by Lewis Edwards whose statue stands in front. Close by the college is Penrhiw, the home of Betsi Cadwaladr, who nursed with Florence Nightingale in the Crimea.

Thomas Charles (1755-1814), whose statue stands outside Capel Tegid in the street of that name just off the high street, was a prominent Methodist Minister who was instrumental in founding the Welsh Sunday Schools, the British and Foreign Bible Society and assisted in translating many religious books, including the Bible, into Welsh. It was from him that Mary Jones obtained her Bible (see Link 5 [13]).

The Welsh community in Patagonia was founded by the Rev. Michael Jones when a Minister here.

In the eighteenth century one of the principal sources of income was the knitting of stockings by both men and women. In 1747 they were producing 1,600 pairs a week, and George III would wear no other.

The Town Council produce an excellent illustrated Town Walk, covering the many interesting buildings which make up Bala.

11. Llanuwchllyn: Caer Gai, the Roman fort just before the village, lies on the Roman road from Chester *(Deva)*.

Apart from being the terminus of the Bala Lake Railway, the village was the birthplace of O. M. Edwards and his son Ifan ab

Owen Edwards, prominent in support of the Welsh language and the teaching of Welsh in schools. There is a statue to both of them.

Another son of the village was the ardent Welsh Nationalist, Michael Jones, one of the founders of the Welsh colony in Patagonia.

There is little of interest here, apart from the Old School House with the village pump in front.

12. Half a mile (800 m) further along the road, and hidden in the trees on the left, is the unusual St Mark's church (if you come to the school you've missed it). Built at the end of the nineteenth century by Henry Wilson, inspired by William Morris and the Art Nouveau movement, it is of an Italianate design and was built with a bequest from the Rev. Charles Tooth, Chaplain and Founder of St Mark's church in Florence. The altar and pulpit are faced with beaten copper panels and the doors inlaid with mother-of-pearl. The church is usually open during the summer and there is parking on the road just below.

On the opposite side of the road is a lay-by and start of a footpath down the Torrent Walk, alongside the rapid river Clywedog. The walk, a favourite with the Victorians, is just under a mile (1.6 km) in length and is fairly steep but easily negotiated, except perhaps by disabled people. The chasm is tree-lined and boulder-strewn with waterfalls, rapids and pools, and is still a popular walk.

13. Corris Uchaf (*upper Corris*) is an undistinguished quarry village compared with its more attractive twin in the valley a mile further on. The area abounds with abandoned quarries and mines, as witness the ugly spoil heaps, though many are being hidden by the Forestry Commission. Between the two Corrises is a craft centre displaying all the usual goods. Also here is King Arthur's Labyrinth, a network of tunnels deep into the mountain with an Arthurian theme. Part of the tour is by boat and a short walk while audio-visual displays recount the tales. Remember it can be quite chilly underground. An unusual attraction worthy of a visit. There is ample free parking, toilets and a café.

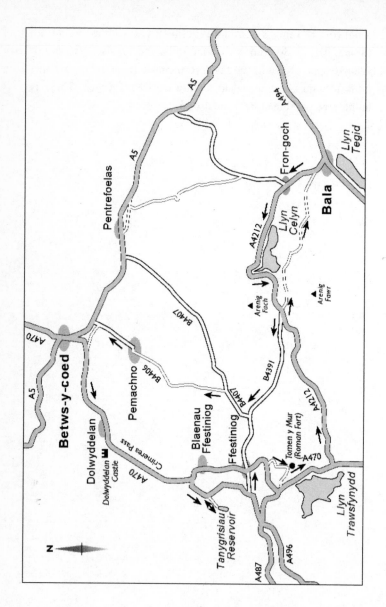

Link 7

Bala – Betws-y-coed – Bala

Distance: 70 miles (112 kilometers)
Time: 3 hours plus stops

Description

There is rather more main road driving on this link than others but it is a run of contrasts; from open moors to wooded valleys and rushing rivers; from old industrial sites to those of the present day and for good measure a little history.

Leave Bala on the A4212 ⇨ Trawsfynydd and Porthmadog (i.e. from the northern end from the main street). This road follows the river Tryweryn, and in 3 miles (4.8 km) passes through the tiny hamlet of Fron-goch (1). Further on we come to the big dam holding back the waters of Llyn Celyn (2). There are several lay-bys overlooking the lake with the mountain Arenig Fawr in the background, and at the far end a picnic area with toilets. After a couple of miles (3.2 km) fork right on the B4391 ⇨ Ffestiniog. A short distance along the road dips to cross tiny river Tai Hirion by Pont Tai Hirion and just up to the right is an old packhorse bridge. The road now enters a forest before opening out onto moorland. The prominent mountains in front are the Moelwyn range on the other side of the Vale of Ffestiniog and back on the left the Cader Idris range. Take the next road on the right (B4407) ⇨ Ysbyty Ifan and Penmachno (3). A mile (1.6 km) or so further on take the minor open road on the left ⇨ Penmachno, by an ancient well, Ffynnon Eidda, rebuilt in 1846. Just before this single track road begins its steep descent, by the cattle grid, a footpath on the right leads up to

Llyn Conwy, the source of Afon Conwy. The road, as it enters Gwydir Forest Park, drops more gently to the valley. The trees here are more widely spaced so there are glimpses of Afon y Foel down in Cwm Hafodyredwydd. Shortly after leaving the forest, give way at the T-junction by the phone box and bear right in this hamlet of Carrog. (The road to the left leads up Cwm Penmachno and is a dead end, but nevertheless a short diversion of interest.) In 0.5 of a mile (800 m) the road crosses to the other side, of what is now the river Machno, by an old bridge. Next we come to the village of Penmachno itself (4), in the centre of which follow the road round to the right ⇨ Betws-y-coed (left ⇨ Tŷ Mawr).

Just over a mile further on, up on the right is Ty'n-y-coed Uchaf, a restored traditional nineteenth-century smallholding owned by the National Trust, but according to their latest handbook now closed. If and when it will re-open is not known. A little further on, opposite converted Chapel Cottages, turn left. This narrow road leads past the now closed woollen mill dated 1839, to Roman Bridge over the fast flowing torrent of the river Machno. This pretty road through the trees, with views down below of the river and, first the Machno Falls and then the Conwy Falls, where the two rivers join to become just the river Conwy. A mile (1.6 km) further on, by a terrace of cottages, there is a track up to the left which is an alternative route to Tŷ Mawr (2.5 miles).

The road now drops down, through the picturesque Fairy Glen, to cross the river Lledr by an old bridge to join the main A470. Turn right and then a right and a left bend over the river Conwy by the Fairy Falls Hotel. On the left is the entrance lodge to Coedycelyn, a mansion used during the last war as a hospital, and later as a base for the Welsh rock band Melys. A sharp right and then immediately left on the A5 London to Holyhead road, followed by a left bend to cross over the Waterloo bridge into Betws-y-coed (5).

Parking on the road is virtually impossible, but at the second turning on the right, opposite the church, there is usually room to park at the railway station complex of shops, cafes, toilets and miniature railway museum, as well as trains to Llandudno and Blaenau Ffestiniog.

Return journey

Leaving the station, turn left on the main road, and at the second turning branch off right up the narrow road by what is currently 'Rock Bottom' camping shop. This attractive tree-lined road passes under the railway bridge and then follows the river Conwy to join the A470(T) and turn right following what is to become the Lledr. This is the main trunk road linking Llandudno and the northern Wales coast with Cardiff, and is currently being upgraded. Consequently you may be subject to delays, though the worst now seems to be over. A feature of the road works is the fine stone walling, showing that craftsmanship is not dead.

We shall be following this road for ten miles (16 km) to Blaenau Ffestiniog. The road passes under Owen Gethin Jones's ornate, castellated, nineteenth-century railway viaduct (known as 'Gethin's viaduct'). We follow this lovely valley, with the railway now on the other side of the river, to the village of Dolwyddelan (6). Breasting the rise out of the village the imposing remains of Dolwyddelan Castle come into view, guarding the gap in the valley – there is a car park on the right. The road now starts the steady climb up to the Crimea Pass (7), before descending steeply to Blaenau Ffestiniog (8).

At the roundabout at the entrance to the town, turn right on the A496 and in 1.5 miles (2.4 km) turn right into the Tanygrisiau Power Station (9) where there is parking, a café and toilets.

Returning to the road, turn right and follow downhill, turning left ⇨ Manod after a mile (1.6 km). This road rises through a wood and in just under 0.5 mile (800 m), as it emerges from the trees take the narrow road that goes down to the right. This pleasant road soon joins the main A470 and turn right to reach the village of Ffestiniog (10) (not to be confused with Blaenau of that name). Entering the village take the very sharp left U-turn ⇨ Dolgellau A470. It is difficult to believe that this is the main road from north to south Wales! Carry on through the village and under the railway bridge, after which the road drops down with pleasant views over the valley. At the bottom of the hill the road crosses the river Cynfal by a phone box, and then starts to rise gently. There is a picnic site here on the banks of the river. In 500 yards (450 m) look out for a narrow road on the left into the forest with a height restriction of 9' 0". This road winds through the forest, rising slowly until it emerges over a cattle grid into open heath. Follow the road down past the TV mast to turn right over a cattle grid, after which there is a parking lay-by on the left. This is the site of Tomen y Mur (11), a Roman encampment on their road Sarn Helen.

Dropping down, pass under the railway bridge, to join the A470 again. Turning left follow the main road for 3 miles (4.8 km) passing, en route, the Trawsfynydd Nuclear Power Station (now being decommissioned) (see Link 4 [16]).

The road by-passes the village of Trawsfynydd. Take the main road on the left, the A4212 ⇨ Bala. This quite fast, pleasant road follows the valley of Cwm Prysor. Notice the disused railway line with arched viaducts clinging to the mountainside high above on the left which will follow the road all the way to Bala. The small lake on the right is Llyn Tryweryn, which feeds the river of that name and which further on was dammed to make Llyn Celyn reservoir.

But before the reservoir, where the B4391 comes in on the left take the minor road opposite ⇨ Arenig, Llidiardau and Rhyduchaf. This attractive very quiet road at first follows the old railway line passing the disused quarry and cluster of cottages of Arenig (12) and then, as Llyn Celyn comes into sight it turns south behind Mynydd Nodol to meander through the countryside to eventually regain the A4212 just 0.75 mile (1.2 km) out of Bala, so turn right to get back into the town.

For a detailed heritage, full-colour guide to this area see **Welcome to Betws-y-coed**, (available in five language). Also the book *'Fron-goch and the birth of the IRA'* by Lyn Ebenezer (www.carreg-gwalch.com).

1. For such a small place, one shop and a handful of houses, Fron-goch has achieved a surprising notoriety over the years. In 1880 a distillery was established to produce Welsh whisky, much to the horror of the local Non-conformists, of whom there were many; it closed down in 1900. In 1915 it housed a German POW camp. In 1916 it was used to house nearly two thousand Irish rebels arrested after the Easter Rising. The inmates formed what was to become the IRA and the internment camp became an 'university of revolution' with military style training.

In the 1970s the shopkeeper hit the headlines when he waged a running battle over several years with the Snowdonia National Park authorities over their refusal to allow a sign offering ice cream!

A quarter of a mile up the road is the Tryweryn National Whitewater Centre, where the volume of water in the river can be controlled from the outlet of Llyn Celyn reservoir, thus giving uniformity of conditions for canoe and rafting competitions. One can watch the exciting events from the riverbanks. It was here that the police came looking for the London train bombers in 2006!

2. The highly controversial Llyn Celyn reservoir was built by

Liverpool Corporation in the 1960s, enforced by a Westminster bill against the will of the vast majority of the Welsh people. Water is fed into the river Tryweryn from where it flows down to join the river Dee at Bala to be abstracted later in Cheshire and then piped to Liverpool. A boulder by the dam commemorates the meeting of Quakers in a now drowned farm prior to emigrating to America. Further along the lakeside is a tiny chapel built to replace that which, along with houses, was flooded. At times of drought the remains of the buildings along with a bridge over what was the Tryweryn appear out of the water.

3. If, instead of turning right, one goes straight ahead for ¾ mile (1.2 km) and over a cattle grid there is a small car park and viewpoint on the left. From here there are magnificent views down into the deep chasm of Cwm Cynfal with its waterfalls, and far across to the sea beyond Porthmadog. There are several of these viewpoints around the area provided by the Rees Jeffrys Road Fund – the man himself having lived from 1872 until 1954 and presumably being a great admirer of the countryside. This little diversion is well worthwhile, but do be careful when leaving the car park to return to the junction, as the road to the left has a blind spot.

4. In this little quarry village the road to the left leads, through forests, to Tŷ Mawr in the remote but beautiful Wybrnant valley. In this medieval farmhouse was born Bishop William Morgan (1540-1604) who translated the entire Bible into Welsh and arranged its publication in 1588. It is a classic translation, giving a new life to an old literary language, and marks the beginning of modern prose in Welsh. A copy was sent to every church in Wales, and all the parishioners became familiar with standard, classical Welsh.

He was educated at Cambridge and is buried at St Asaph, where he became bishop. The property, now owned by the National Trust, is open to the public. There is an exhibition and a short trail through the adjoining forest.

5. To enter Betws-y-coed, cross Telford's cast iron bridge which bears the inscription: 'This arch was constructed in the same year as the Battle of Waterloo was fought'. Betws-y-coed, standing at the crossroads of the A5 London to Holyhead road and the A470 artery to central and southern Wales, has always been a busy village and one used to catering for travellers. That, and the magnificent scenery, account for the present-day tourists who arrive in their thousands.

The village and its surroundings have always been popular with artists, and a colony became established in the mid nineteenth century. The sign painted for the Royal Oak Hotel by the water colourist David Cox can be seen inside the hotel.

The Snowdonia National Park Information Centre is based in Y Stablau (*the stables*) in the centre of the village, and keeps a comprehensive range of leaflets, guides and audiovisual displays. The village is almost entirely devoted to the tourist and there are plenty of restaurants and cafes, as well as higher-class gift shops and those catering for all outdoor activities. There is a miniature railway and vintage car museum by the station.

The fourteenth-century church is situated behind the station and is probably the oldest building in Betws.

6. Dolwyddelan: this unremarkable village lies in a beautiful setting. A little sixteenth-century church to the left has many interesting artefacts. However, the village's claim to fame is its castle, which is situated just beyond the village, and occupies a strategic position on a hill guarding the pass between Moel Siabod and Moel Pen-y-bryn. Built in the early thirteenth century by Llywelyn Fawr (*the Great*), the castle was involved in the struggle between the Welsh and Edward I, to whom it fell in 1283. It was then abandoned, only to be occupied by Maredudd ab Ieuan, descended from the Princes of Powys, in the fifteenth century.

Since it stands right beside the road it is easy to make a quick visit to appreciate the stunning setting. The castle is in the care of CADW.

7. Crimea pass: the origin of the name is uncertain but probably after a pub of that name, maybe itself named after the Crimean War, which stood in the lay-by, and which was no doubt well-patronised by the many quarrymen who worked in the area. At this point the railway enters a 2 mile (3.2 km) tunnel under Moel Dyrnogydd before arriving in Blaenau Ffestiniog.

8. Blaenau Ffestiniog: depressing though the approach is, the town is full of interest. It was developed in the mid nineteenth century to exploit the vast reserves of high quality slate. The results of the quarrymens' labours are all too clearly seen; unfortunately, for every ton of good slate, more than ten times that amount is produced as spoil, which had to be dumped somewhere with little regard to the visual impact.

The award-winning Llechwedd slate caverns are well worth a visit to appreciate the hardship under which the men worked. Wonder at the vast caverns hacked out by hand. The underground lake has been used in films. Also in the complex is a Victorian village with pub and shops where re-minted Victorian coins have to be used, after being exchanged at the 'bank'. There is a café, as well as a shop, pub and licensed restaurant.

At the other end of the town are the Manod quarries where,

during the last war, Britain's art treasures were moved from the National Gallery in London and stored deep underground in specially air-conditioned chambers. The task of getting some of the largest pictures up the steep and narrow 'roads' presented many problems.

In the centre of the town the Ffestiniog narrow gauge railway shares a specially created station with the main line trains from Llandudno. The demise of the slate industry can be seen everywhere, though strenuous efforts are being made, with some success, to promote the town as a tourist centre and to attract light industry.

One unusual feature is that the town boasts the only Russian Orthodox church in Snowdonia!

9. The Ffestiniog Hydro-Electric Scheme is perhaps the main attraction here. During off-peak times water is pumped from Tanygrisiau reservoir up to Llyn Stwlan storage dam, high up on Moel Mawr, to be released to drive the generators below at times of heavy demand. There is an attractive car park, together with popular café and toilets. A private road rises 1,000 feet (300 m) to the upper stwlan dam, from were the views are magnificent.

This is a village of contrasts – in front, beautiful countryside, behind, the spoil heaps of disused quarries. The village itself has a certain charm and there are many walks, both long and short, from here, and there is a station on the Ffestiniog Railway.

10. Ffestiniog: the former quarry workers' cottages have been improved, and it is now a pleasant little village in a glorious setting and thus a desirable place to live. There are many walks from here including a short one to see Rhaeadr Cynfal (*waterfall*), just south of the village.

11. Tomen y Mur: this first century AD Roman fort was an important staging post on Sarn Helen, the Roman road which ran south from here to where it was crossed by the road that ran from the fort at Caer Gai near Bala to Segontium at Caernarfon. The site, which unfortunately is on private land, was fairly extensive, even boasting a small amphitheatre. In the centre of the site is a mound, once a Norman motte.

12. Arenig: the two Arenig mountains lie astride the A4212 with Arenig Fach to the north and Arenig Fawr to the south. Both are well over 2,000 feet (600 m), with the latter one being the more dramatic: at the summit, there is a plaque to commemorate the Flying Fortress which crashed into the mountain in 1943, killing all eight US crew members.

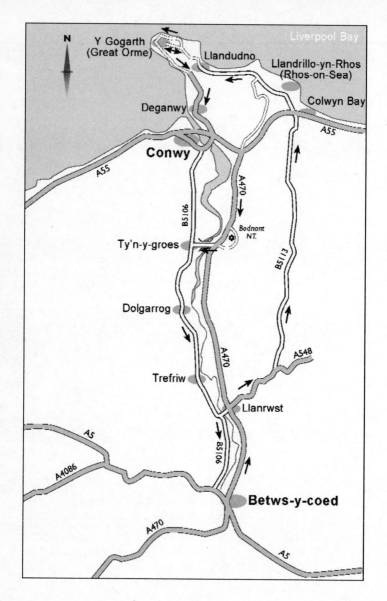

Link 8

Betws-y-coed – Conwy – Betws-y-coed

Distance: 56 miles (90 kilometers)
Time: 3 hours plus stops

Description

This is a journey through time – Bronze and Iron Ages, the Romans, Middle Ages, the Victorian years through to the present day, with a trip to the seaside thrown in for good measure, and all within some magnificent scenery. The driving is easy, following both sides of the river Conwy, and at 56 miles (90 km) is one of the shortest routes, but then there is plenty to see and explore.

Leave Betws-y-coed on the main A5 heading south. Immediately after crossing the Waterloo bridge, on the edge of the village, turn left on the A470 ⇨ Llanrwst and Llandudno. Keep going for 4 miles (6.4 km) to Llanrwst (1). In the centre of the town, turn right on the A548 ⇨ Abergele. The road rises steadily, with many twists and turns, for 2.5 miles (4 km), and nearly at the top of the rise take the minor road on the left, the B5113 ⇨ Colwyn Bay. There are fine views on both sides. Continue, ignoring all roads coming in from either side, for just over 8 miles (12.8 km), where there are magnificent views on the left to the Conwy estuary just before entering Bryn-y-maen (2). The road now starts to descend to the coast as the environs of Colwyn Bay are reached. One and a half miles (2.4 km) after Bryn-y-maen the road takes a sharp right hand bend ⇨ Colwyn Bay B5113. In 500 yards (450 m) follow the road down to the left through a wooded valley until, at the bottom of the hill, a 'No Entry' sign forces a right turn. The property around here is part of Rydal-Penrhos College.

Next take the fifth road on the left, Pwll-y-Crochan Avenue. At the mini roundabout (3) go straight ahead, and then crossing another main road, pass under the expressway and railway bridges to arrive on the promenade (4). Turn left and continue along the sea front, where there is ample free parking, to Rhos-on-sea (5). Still keeping to the sea front you will come to Penrhyn Bay (6), with the golf course on the left and the great limestone outcrop of the Little Orme in front. The road rises slightly as it veers away from the sea, with houses now on both sides leading to a roundabout. Take the fourth exit up the dual carriageway hill. At the top the road now becomes a single carriageway, bearing right and then left when the impressive 3 mile (5 km) sweep of Llandudno Bay (7) comes into view. Continue along the promenade where there is plenty of free parking at this end, but becomes 'Pay and Display' half-way along. The main shopping area, Mostyn Street, runs almost parallel to the promenade and can be reached down any of the side streets. There is a multi-storey car park on the other side of the main street.

At the far end of the promenade, by the pier entrance, take the second exit at the roundabout and then, opposite the front entrance to the Grand Hotel, take the narrow colonnaded road up to the left, which will eventually reach the summit of Y Gogarth (*the Great Orme*) (8). First it leads into Happy Valley gardens with a view down to the pier. Continue up through the gardens. At first sight one wonders whether one should be driving through the park, but carry on over a cattle grid onto the car park for the artificial ski slope and toboggan run. There is a pub and all the usual facilities.

In the top car park go through the open gate on the left onto the metalled narrow road and follow down to the traffic lights and crossing the tram track, turn right. (This gate is usually open, but in the unlikely event of it being locked return to the roundabout by the pier head, go straight across up the one-way street and at the top turn right by the Empire Hotel signposted to the summit. There is a sharp hairpin bend at the start and the gradient is steep and later the road has to be shared with the tramway.)

The climb to the summit is fairly steep to start with, but levels out at the tram half-way station. On the left is the entrance to the Bronze Age copper mines. The summit 'Pay and Display' car park is soon reached. The views from here are magnificent and the air very 'fresh'! The Summit Complex, with two communication masts, houses all the facilities one would expect – eating, drinking and playing.

Returning back down the road turn left just before the half-way station, crossing the tramlines. A little further on there is ample free parking on the grass, with picnic tables. Carry on down the hill passing the little St Trillo church, and after a couple of hairpin bends come out onto the Marine Drive. There is a toll to pay but it is money well spent. It is a one-way road so turn left. This fine road climbs, clinging to the cliff edge, to another car park and café. Down below is the lighthouse, no longer in use as such, as it is now a B&B. As the road sweeps down and round the headland so the views unfold, from Puffin Island off Anglesey, round to Conwy with the backdrop of mountains.

At the bottom, where the houses start, take care as the road now becomes two-way. The road comes out onto the West Shore (9) at Penmorfa. There is free parking on the promenade and a 'Pay and Display' at the far end, where of necessity turn left then right to the far end by the sand dunes, and left to join the main road. Turn right and carry on, passing through Deganwy (10) to eventually come to a roundabout. Take the third exit to cross the bridge into Conwy (11).

At the mini-roundabout take the second exit to enter the one-way system. There is a short stay car park on the left and another by the station a little further on – both are 'Pay and Display'. If stopping for a longer period then at the mini-roundabout turn left alongside the castle, and pass under the town walls to follow the road round to the right where there is a much bigger park. There are footpaths leading up the to town.

Return journey

Starting from Lancaster Square take the street up beside the police station and through the narrow archway under the town walls. Keep on going till the road bears right to cross over the A55 expressway and then take the slip road on the right ⇨ Chester (going straight ahead leads to the marina and picnic area overlooking the river). Take care joining the traffic as the expressway is busy and vehicles travelling fast. The road dips down to pass through the tunnel under the river (12). Emerging from the tunnel continue as far as Junction 19 ⇨ Betws-y-coed and Bodnant. Take the fourth exit under the expressway on the A470 and at the next roundabout, by the Black Cat petrol station take the third exit, the A470 ⇨ Betws-y-coed. At the top of the hill, 0.5 mile (800 m) further on is a lay-by on the right with seats and views across the river to Conwy Castle and the mountains beyond. For those interested in gardening there are a number of centres along this stretch of road. Firstly the Snowdonia Nurseries on the right on entering Glan Conwy with its views across the estuary. At the top of the hill out of Glan Conwy there is a restored water mill.

A mile (1.6 km) further on a narrow road on the right leads to Aberconwy Nurseries, where Dr Lever, botanist, specialises in alpines; across the road is the Talgoed garden centre. Having risen, the road now drops down through woods and on the left, well-signposted, is the road leading to the National Trust's Bodnant Gardens (13). There is ample free parking on the left, though the gardens are extremely popular. A café and toilets adjoin the car park. Continuing past the gardens in 0.5 mile (800 m) turn right by the bus shelter and phone box ⇨ A470. The house in front was formerly the Sun Inn. This narrow road drops down to the valley, over a bridge and starts to rise then branch off to the left on a narrower lane ⇨ Tal-y-cafn (don't be misled into carrying on ⇨ A470). As this road rises look out for the aerial view of the Conwy river on the right. Next the road drops fairly steeply to the A470. Taking great care, for the traffic is fast. Cross over to go down beside the Tal-y-cafn pub ⇨ Ty'n-y-groes, Dolgarrog and station. Go over the level crossing by the station and then cross the river Conwy on a metal bridge. Taking the road to the left, follow it a further mile (1.6 km) to meet the B5106 in the village of Ty'n-y-groes and turn left.

In just under a mile (1.6 km) a lane on the left signposted 'Cemetery' leads to the Roman Fort of Caerhun (14) and a little church. Next pass through the village of Tal-y-bont (15). From hereon the road is squeezed between the flood plain of the Conwy and the sheer, tree-covered escarpment that comes right down to the road. On the left is the string of houses that is Dolgarrog (16). Next comes the Trefriw Roman Spa (17). The actual village of Trefriw is a little further on (18).

In 2 miles (3.2 km) the straight major road on the left leads directly to Llanrwst, but bear right with the B5106 ⇨ Betws-y-coed. On the left is the historical Gwydir Castle (19), open to the public, and on the right a little further on, a track leads up to Gwydir Uchaf Chapel (20), also open to the public. Here also is the Gwydir Forest Park centre with exhibition, car park and picnic area.

The final three mile (4.8 km) run into Betws-y-coed is a most attractive road with the forest on the right and the river down below on the left. Entering the village there is a 'Pay and Display' car park, toilets and picnic area on the banks of the river just to the right before Pont-y-Pair (bridge of the cauldron) crosses the river Llugwy. At this point the fast-flowing river tumbles over the rocks before a waterfall under the five-arch bridge. Turn left down the main street.

For detailed heritage, full-colour guides to this area see **Welcome to Betws-y-coed** and **Welcome to Conwy**, (available in five languages), and **Welcome to Llandudno**, (www.carreg-gwalch.com).

1. Llanrwst is a pleasant market town noted for its clock- and harp-making, printing, and tannery, the latter now having been turned into a language centre, craft centre and bistro.

The elegant three-arched bridge, Pont Fawr, seen on entering the town may possibly have been designed by Inigo Jones, the famous architect. Across the bridge is a fifteenth-century stone cottage, once the courthouse and now a café, owned and let by the National Trust.

St Grwst, the parish church, though not particularly old, has a fine rood screen, and loft. Adjoining the church is Gwydir Chapel, with large stone coffin, stone effigy of a knight and several brasses. There is a row of seventeenth-century almshouses, now a museum. This is the home town of William Salisbury, who, in the mid sixteenth century, compiled the first Welsh/English dictionary and first translated the New Testament into Welsh.

2. In Bryn-y-maen there is a fine church, built in 1897 to the design of John Douglas, the Chester architect, and founded by Eleanor Jones, who, born into poverty, by dint of hard work and education, married Charles Frost, heir to the Bryn-y-maen estate, to whose memory she built the church.

Beyond the church is the RSPCA centre for the area.

3. Those wishing to visit the town centre of Colwyn Bay should turn right here. The arrival of the railway in 1848 quickly turned the village of Old Colwyn into a popular holiday resort and residential area for the wealthy, as will be seen from the many large fine houses. The town, which once boasted some of the finest shops in northern Wales, has unfortunately gone downmarket. It has lost its popularity as a holiday resort to neighbouring Llandudno, and the marvellous three miles of fine clean sand is more often as not deserted. No longer are staff available to run these desirable residences, and they are increasingly being converted into superior flats or nursing homes, whilst the former hotels and B&Bs are let as bed-sits. But in spite of this the town still has a lot to offer; strong efforts are being made to reverse the trend, and Colwyn Bay frequently wins prizes for its floral displays.

During the last war the town played host to the Ministry of Food and parts of the BBC.

There is a very good, fifty-acre sports complex on the edge of town and the Welsh Mountain Zoo has a good reputation. The expressway means that Manchester and Liverpool are not much more than an hour away, and through trains run to London.

Apart from all this, Colwyn Bay is a good centre for exploring the mountains of Snowdonia.

4. Looking to the right is the pier, built in 1900, burnt down in 1922, and again in 1933, which has in its day hosted many well-known artistes. The present building is rather an eyesore and in need of complete renovation, the present owner is doing his best but it needs a lot of money spending on it – perhaps the council or some other authority should help out.

Beyond the pier, at Penmaenhead, in 1399, Richard II was ambushed, after returning from a campaign in Ireland. Taken to

Flint Castle, he was forced to abdicate by Henry Bolingbroke who later became Henry IV. Further round beyond the headland, in the distance is Rhyl, offshore of which can be seen, on a clear day, the wind farm. Further round still, on the horizon, a gas rig. The large block of retirement flats on the right is known locally as Colditz! Timothy Dalton, who played James Bond in two films, was born in Colwyn Bay.

5. Llandrillo-yn-Rhos (*Rhos-on-sea*) also had a pier once, 1,500 feet (450 m) long, and bought second-hand from Douglas in the Isle of Man, in 1895.

At one time there were regular sailings from Liverpool to the northern coast of Wales, calling at Rhos. In 1908 the steamship *Rhosneigr* sank whilst trying to dock. Some of the wreckage can be seen at very low tide, as can the remains of the old fishing weir established by the monks in the thirteenth century and still in use at the beginning of the twentieth century when, in 1907, 10 tons of mackerel were caught in a single tide.

The Caley Arms Hotel and promenade were named after the Caley family, one of whom, Sir George, designed a practical flying machine fifty years before the Wright brothers, and in 1853 built a machine that would carry a man for about 300 yards (300 m).

The village itself has a number of better class shops and eating establishments. The Harlequin Puppet Theatre is the only purpose-built marionette theatre in Britain. Just beyond Rhos Point on the promenade, but out of sight from the road, is the tiny St Trillo's Chapel – measuring just 8 ft by 11 ft (240 cm x 335 cm) it can seat six people, and is thought to be the smallest in Britain. Named after the sixth-century Celtic saint it is built over an ancient well and is usually unlocked during the day.

Further along the promenade we come to a house with rather an odd name: No. 147 is called The Old Budget Gate. The local landowner, Mr Horton, was so incensed by Lloyd George's land tax to pay for his introduction of the Old Age Pension in 1909 that he erected a toll gate on what was then an unmade road; cars were charged a shilling and prams a penny. This toll continued under the Tramway Company, whose line ran from Llandudno to Colwyn Bay, until finally abolished in 1963 when the council adopted the road.

The prominent sixteenth-century church inland was once painted white to serve as a landmark for sailors. The unusual square tower in the corner of the main tower, known locally as the Rector's chair, served as a lookout, and was part of a chain of signalling posts along the coast to warn of pirate attacks - which were prevalent in the seventeenth century. The churchyard contains the grave of Harold Lowe, a heroic officer on the *Titanic*.

The distinctive hill behind Rhos is Bryn Euryn, a nature reserve. From the summit the views are wide, which explains why the RAF took it over during the war as an early radar station. At the foot of the hill are the ruins of a manor house built by Ednyfed Fychan, chief adviser to Llywelyn Fawr and one of whose descendants was Owain Tudur, grandfather of Henry VII.

6. The private house just before the golf course bears a plaque on the garden wall (not on view to the general public), stating that 'Prince Madog sailed from here Abercerrig-gwynion in 1170 AD and landed in Mobile, Alabama with his ships Corn Gwynant and *Pedre Sant*'. A similar plaque has been placed on the shores of Mobile Bay. If this legend is correct, then he discovered America 322 years before Columbus. At that time the river, which crosses the golf course, was wider and navigable and there was probably a small harbour, the stones of which probably constitute the rockery and garden wall.

It was on what is now the golf course that on 10 August, 1910 Robert Lorraine, actor and aviator landed his Farmer Racer bi-plane. He had intended flying from Blackpool to Holyhead and then on to Ireland but was forced to land here, becoming the first plane to land in Wales.

The retirement bungalows and houses of Penrhyn Bay nestle below the massive outcrop of limestone – The Little Orme. It is but a shadow of its former self, huge bites having been taken out to be shipped, from a quay below, to feed the blast furnaces of Scotland.

With the persecution of the Catholics in the sixteenth century, Father William Davies of Penrhyn Old Hall set up a printing press in a cave on the seaward side of the Orme. Here he printed the first Welsh book to be produced in Wales, *Y Drych Cristianogawl*, in 1586. Denounced by Sir Thomas Mostyn, local landowner, he was hanged for treason in Beaumaris castle in 1593, and subsequently beatified by the Pope in 1987.

More recently the quarry was used as an artillery practice range during the last war and a film set for *Far from the Madding Crowd*.

7. Llandudno works hard to maintain its Victorian image and thus is devoid of all the usual clutter associated with most seaside resorts. You can still hire a deck chair to listen to the band; take a trip round the bay; have a donkey ride; watch Professor Codman's Punch and Judy show; take a walk on the pier. The gently sweeping promenade and gardens are backed by colourful, elegant hotels culminating in the Victorian pier built in 1876. Many famous musicians have performed with the orchestra which was a feature at the end of the pier: Thomas Beecham, Adrian Boult, and Malcolm Sargent all played and conducted here.

Between the wars the steamship companies ran a regular service from Liverpool and excursion trips to the Isle of Man. Some years ago a cruise liner, anchored in the bay, was unable to embark its passengers after a trip to Snowdonia, due to adverse weather, and they were rescued by the lifeboat and accommodated overnight. The following year the liner returned and wishing to repay the hospitality invited the civic dignitaries and lifeboat crew to dinner aboard. When they came to disembark the weather had worsened, and they ended up being taken to the Isle of Man, to return by air the following day!

The main shopping street, which runs just behind the promenade, has not been vandalised by the usual stores which make every high street look the same, and it is still possible to browse in comfort under the glass-canopied shop windows. A new shopping complex has just been completed which will make Llandudno the premier shopping centre for northern Wales, though some of the smaller traders may suffer as a result.

Whilst strolling around the town take time to look above the level of the shop windows at the fascinating architecture of the buildings, the cast iron verandas and Victorian street furniture. The Mostyn family, whose foresight developed the town in the 1840s, still keep a strict but sympathetic eye on developments: for example, building heights are not allowed to exceed the width of the street. An electric tramway, closed in 1956, ran down the main street and to Colwyn Bay.

The Grand Theatre, which was opened in 1901 and from where the BBC, during the war, broadcast such programmes as 'ITMA', is now a night club and replaced by a new theatre and conference centre on the promenade which features international orchestras, the Welsh National Opera operas and assorted concerts.

There is a small museum in the town established with a legacy from Francis Chardon who made a fortune in India out of indigo.

Another item of interest is the 'Home Front Experience', which shows how the civilian population fared during the Second World War. There is also a small art gallery.

An interesting visitor to the resort in the 1880s was Queen Elizabeth of Romania, who stayed at the Marine Hotel for some time, during which she fully entered into the life of the local community. She wrote novels and poems under the pen name Carmen Silva.

8. The Great Orme: this massive limestone outcrop rises to a height of 685 ft (209 m). There are four ways to the top: by car, the route given previously; on foot, via three waymarked trails; by cable car, starting from behind the café in Happy Valley Gardens; and by the Great Orme Tramway starting from Church Walks.

The Orme is a designated Country Park and Nature Reserve and has many interesting features. There are over 400 types of plants, some very rare; butterflies; and breeding colonies of sea birds. The feral Kashmir goats, which roam freely, were a present from Queen Victoria, who received the original stock as a present from the Shah of Persia at her coronation. There are now over 200 of them. There have been some complaints so maybe the Queen was glad to be rid of them!

The Happy Valley Gardens, where open-air entertainment was provided for the visitors, were laid out in 1888. The cable car ascent, which is the longest in Britain and gives a bird's eye view of the Orme, Llandudno and the Conwy estuary, starts from near the café (there is very limited parking). Close by is that old favourite of the Victorians, the 'camera obscura'. The artificial ski slope and 700 m long Cresta Toboggan run are popular with young and old alike.

The Great Orme Tramway, the only cable-hauled tramway operating on public roads, was opened in 1902 and still uses the original carriages, each named after a Saint. In 1932 a carriage broke loose, with one fatality. Apart from that incident it has a good safety record. At the half-way station, where passengers have to change trams, there is an interesting museum.

Archaeological exploration of the Bronze Age Copper mines have pre-dated anything previously known, and parts are now proved to have been mined 4,000 years ago. There are guided tours of the site, including the underground caverns. There is an exhibition, tearoom, and shop. The summit complex was once one of the chain of telegraph stations linking Caergybi (*Holyhead*) with Liverpool, and a message from the former would be received by the latter in 5 minutes! It now houses a visitor centre, restaurant, bar, and shops. It was once owned by Randolph Turpin, the boxer. The views from here are spectacular, if a little breezy. On a clear day the Lakeland mountains are visible as well, of course, as those of Snowdonia beyond the estuary of the Conwy. The Menai Strait, Puffin Island, and the east coast of Ynys Môn (*Anglesey*) appear to be but a stone's throw away.

In 1939, in Liverpool Bay, the submarine *Thetis*, on trials, with her builders, Cammell Lairds of Birkenhead, sank inexplicably with the loss of all aboard save five. She was later salvaged and at HMS Thunderbolt had a good war record before being sunk again.

The tiny twelfth-century St Tudno's church was built on a site that goes back to the sixth century. A storm in 1839 severely damaged the roof and it was abandoned for fifteen years, during which time the locals helped themselves to whatever was available! In 1855 it was restored and re-opened for services. The open air services are extremely popular on Sundays during the summer. The 4.5 mile (7.2 km) Marine Drive was built in 1878 and is a toll road. The lighthouse was built in 1862, and at 352 ft (90 m) above sea level was the highest in Wales, until it became redundant in 1985

131

and turned into a guesthouse. Continuing around the Marine Drive, below the road are the remains of a large artillery training range from World War Two.

9. Llandudno is fortunate to have two beaches and this, the West Shore, is less touristy, but it faces south, has glorious views, and a good stretch of sand. Its chief claim to fame is its association with Alice in Wonderland. The story goes that Alice, daughter of Henry Liddell, came here to their holiday home, 'Penmorfa', and it was there that Charles Dodgson, a family friend, who wrote under the name of Lewis Carroll, met her and based his stories on Alice. There is some doubt that he ever came to Llandudno, and it is thought that the setting was, in fact, Oxford. Nevertheless a memorial White Rabbit was erected in 1933 on the promenade and unveiled by Lloyd George. Unfortunately vandalism has caused a metal cage to be erected round the memorial. Penmorfa itself was demolished at the end of 2008 to make way for flats.

This was once the industrial area of Llandudno for the processing of copper from the mines on the Orme and remains of an adit can be seen from Abbey Place.

10. On the Vardre, the hill behind Deganwy, are the remains of a thirteenth-century Welsh castle, fought over by both the Welsh and the English. It was destroyed by Llywelyn Fawr in 1257. Edward I built a bigger and better one on the other side of the river!

The small harbour was built by the railway company in the forlorn hope of obtaining a share of the slate traffic from Blaenau Ffestiniog. This never materialised, and the harbour fell into disuse for many years before being turned into a marina and hotel complex in 2005.

11. Conwy has one of Edward I's castles built in 1283 by his personal castle builder, James of St George, at a cost of £15,000. He also built the town walls to keep the Welsh out. He thoughtfully included a row of public toilets which emptied into the river Gyffin which fortuitously ran at the foot of the wall at that time! The walls which encircle the town, can be walked round and are worth the slight effort. As part of his plans to colonize Wales Edward relocated the Cistercian monks from their abbey in the town to Maenan further upstream, taking with them the body of Llywelyn; what was the abbey is now St Mary's Parish Church.

There are three bridges on the approach to the town by the easiest route from Chester and England. Until Telford's revolutionary chain suspension bridge, with a span of 327 feet (100 m) was built in 1826, travellers had to make the hazardous ferry crossing. Then in 1849 Stephenson built a bridge to carry the railway from Chester across the river Conwy. He too used a revolutionary design: a single span box construction. Both bridges were forerunners of identical, but longer ones, crossing the Menai Strait.

By the 1950s the volume of traffic demanded a much wider bridge, and in 1958 a single span steel arch bridge was opened. The old suspension bridge is now in the care of the National Trust and open for pedestrian traffic only. There is an exhibition in the old tollhouse which, like both bridges, was designed to harmonise with the castle.

Routing heavy goods traffic through the narrow streets of Conwy had, by the early 1960s, become virtually impossible, and discussions, often acrimonious, began on a third crossing of the river. It was finally decided on a tunnel which duly opened in 1991, by-passing the town completely, much to the relief of the residents.

To be seen within the town walls is Plas Mawr, the finest surviving Elizabethan town house in Britain, built by a wealthy merchant, Robert Wynn and noted for its fine plasterwork. Fully restored, it is in the care of CADW. Behind Plas Mawr is a permanent exhibition of works by the Royal Cambrian Academy of Art; Aberconwy House, a medieval merchant's house (National Trust); a fine statue of Llywelyn in Lancaster Square; a teapot museum in Castle Street; the fourteenth-century St Mary's Church has a tombstone in the churchyard which inspired Wordsworth's poem 'We are Seven'.

Outside the walls, on the quayside, is a mussel museum. From Roman times the mussels were collected for their pearls, one of which is included in the Crown Jewels, but nowadays they are harvested to eat, and the exhibition shows the process of purification.

Also on the quay is Britain's smallest house: 72" (1,830 mm) wide and 122" (3,100 mm) high, it was occupied by a 6' 3" (1,905 mm) fisherman until 1900. Regular boat trips up and down the river sail from here.

Further out is Bodlondeb house and gardens, former home of Albert Wood who made his fortune making the massive anchor chains for the *SS Great Britain*. He gave the house and grounds to the town and it is now the Council Offices, with a tropical butterfly jungle in the garden.

12. The Conwy Tunnel, which finally relieved the town of an increasing amount of through traffic, was built on the 'cut and cover' principle whereby large concrete sections are dropped into a trench in the riverbed. The sections were prefabricated on the site used to make sections of the Mulberry Harbour, so vital for the successful D-Day landings.

The site is now Conwy Marina with a picnic area, housing development, and pub where there is a display depicting the

Mulberry Harbour. Opened in 1991, the tunnel is part of the A55 expressway from Queensferry to Holyhead which is now the accepted route to Ireland.

There is an important RSPB reserve on the estuary – to visit leave at junction 18 at the far end of the tunnel.

13. Bodnant: first established in 1875, the present gardens were given to the National Trust by Lord Aberconwy in 1949. The 80-acre site is noted for azaleas, camellias, magnolias, spring flowers, and of course, the well-known laburnum arch, whilst in the dell there is a good number of specimen trees. The house is not open to the public, but the magnificent vista over the Conwy valley, which the house was built to take advantage of, can be appreciated by all. There is a garden and craft centre as well as a cafeteria the other side of the A470 – connected to the gardens by a pedestrian underpass.

14. Caerhun: the Roman fort of *Kanovium* was probably built in 78 AD to guard the river crossing on the road from *Deva* (Chester) to *Segontium* (Caernarfon). There is a beautiful little church in the corner of the site.

15. This little hamlet is noted for nothing else except the river Dulyn, which drops through a gorge, with waterfall, on its journey from Llyn Eigiau to the river Conwy. A pleasant short walk.

16. On entering Dolgarrog, you will see the site of aluminium works on the left, now closed and subject to redevelopment. They were established in the early twentieth century to make use of the abundant water supply to produce the electricity needed. Unfortunately the dam, high in the hills, burst in 1925, and the raging torrent carried away part of the village, killing sixteen people.

Across the road is a memorial to those killed, and a short walk through the woods beside the river where the huge boulders that came crashing down can be seen.

17. The waters were first discovered by the Romans, and the spa became popular with the Victorians who, in those days, could sail up river from Conwy. The site has been opened up with guided tours of the wells. Samples of the iron rich waters, which are marketed under the trade name 'Spatone' are on sale.

18. The main claim to fame here is the woollen mill, owned by the Williams family for 150 years. The waters of the river Crafnant drive the turbines to power the looms. The process of making Welsh tapestry items is on show, and they are on sale in the shop.

The church is said to have been built by Llywelyn Fawr to save his Princess having to walk up the steep hill to Llanrhychwyn!

19. Gwydir Castle: ancestral home of the Wynn family, descended from the kings of Gwynedd and connected to everyone of substance. Present buildings are from the sixteenth century and are being restored by the present owners. The complete panels of the original dining room were sold many years ago to Randolph Hearst, the American newspaper tycoon, and were subsequently found in a New York storeroom. They have been brought back to their rightful home. The castle is said to be haunted and has a priest hole. Known for its peacocks which wander freely. Open to the public.

20. Private chapel built by Sir John Wynne in 1604. It has fine woodwork and a painted ceiling. The key is available from the nearby Gwydir Forest Park Centre, where there is a car park, picnic area and exhibition.

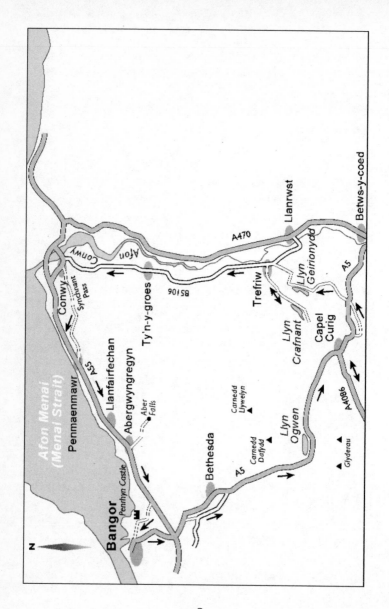

Link 9

Conwy – Bangor – Conwy

Distance: 50 miles (80.5 kilometers)
Time: 3 hours plus stops

Description

At the start, this link follows the coastal plain to Bangor before heading up into the mountains, along an historical road into the heart of Eryri (Snowdonia). The return is through the less popular, but equally scenic, hills and lakes on the west side of the Conwy valley.

From the centre of Conwy, by the statue of Llywelyn, go up beside the police station and take the first street on the left, Upper Gate Street, to pass through the very narrow gateway of the town walls (beware of on-coming traffic). Follow the road round to the right and, leaving the houses behind, come into open country with views of Conwy Mountain on the right. After crossing the cattle grid, beware of the sheep as the road starts to rise up to the Sychnant Pass (1). Further on, just before entering the trees there is a car park on the left – an ideal spot to stretch one's legs. If feeling energetic the climb to the top of the hill beside the car park will give fine views down over Conwy, its river and beyond.

    At the top of the pass there is another small parking place with a magnificent view down through the 'V' formed by the heather-clad slopes of Allt-Wen on the right and Foel-lus on the left, to the Menai Strait and Ynys Môn (*Anglesey*) beyond. There is often an ice cream van parked here in the summer.

    The road now drops very steeply down to the hamlet of Capelulo with its pubs and café, then descends gently down to

Penmaenmawr (2). Carry on to the end of the main street and join the A55 expressway, being careful of the fast approaching traffic from the right.

Go through the Pen-y-clip tunnel to the village of Llanfairfechan (3). Turn left at the roundabout and follow the road round right, but then immediately take the narrow street on the right which leads down, under the road and rail, onto the promenade. At the far end there is ample parking, toilets and a café. Turning left up into the centre of the village, turn right at the traffic lights and shortly rejoin the A55, taking care.

A couple of miles (3.2 km) further on a slip road leads down to the village of Abergwyngregyn (4). If not wishing to visit the falls, for which the village is famous, keep to the expressway.

From the road there is a panoramic view across Traeth Lafan over which, many years ago, people were tempted to take a short cut to Beaumaris, sometimes with tragic results. Two miles (3.2 km) further on leave the main road for the minor road ⇨ Tal-y-bont. The road crosses back over the expressway, and at the 'Give Way' sign turn right. Continue for a further two miles (3.2 km) to where the road skirts the wall of the Penrhyn Castle estate (5). At the roundabout by the entrance to the castle turn right and then go straight ahead to drop down to Port Penrhyn, where there is a car park on the right (6) and on to the centre of the City of Bangor (7).

At the second mini-roundabout, beneath the University, turn sharp left to where there are 'Pay and Display' and multi-storey car parks. There is no clearly defined centre in Bangor for cars, so as a starting and finishing reference point the railway station is as good a place as anywhere. For that option, carry on up the main road and the station is right in front at the top of the hill, by the traffic lights, with a new one-way system.

Return journey

From the station take the main road in front back down, and pass the University on the left. At the far end of this road, the A5, follow as it bends right by the boatyard in front. It is signposted to Betws-y-coed. Back up at the roundabout by the entrance to Penrhyn Castle take the second exit, keeping to the main road. At the next roundabout, over the expressway, continue straight ahead. A sign proclaims that this is a 'historic route', referring to the fact that it was originally engineered by Thomas Telford between 1815 and 1830 as the main road from London to Holyhead, and then by ferry to Dublin. The road now drops down a wooded valley to a bridge over the river Ogwen, but immediately before crossing take the minor road on the right ⇨ Tregarth and then the first left by Dinas Farm caravan site. This road follows the south bank of the river until turning left, where it joins a wider road by a phone box. This road in effect by-passes the town of Bethesda (8) on the opposite side of the river, until it rejoins the A5. The huge Penrhyn slate quarry is up on the right, more or less hidden from view, except for the spoil heaps.

We are now entering Nant Ffrancon (9), the rugged valley that follows the river Ogwen up to its source, Llyn Ogwen. A mile and a half (2.4 km) further along, on the left, is the Snowdonia Mountain Lodge (10). Follow the road as far as the cluster of buildings at the foot of Llyn Ogwen (11). This is the heart of Snowdonia, a Mecca for climbers the world over. The road continues along the edge of the lake, round the towering buttress of Tryfan, and shortly passes the watershed to join the river Llugwy, which is followed, through rather bleak moorland, to gently descend to Capel Curig (12).

Follow the A5 and on the right notice the little tollhouse, a reminder when this was once a turnpike road, before coming to

Cobdens Hotel (13) and then the Ty'n-y-coed Hotel (14). Just after the latter look out for an easily missed narrow road on the right opposite the phone box. This quiet, pretty road cuts out a stretch of the busy A5, and after crossing the river on a high bridge, Pont Cyfyng, drops down to follow it for a couple of miles (3.2 km) (15) before rejoining the A5 again.

Turning left, cross the main road bridge and take the minor road going up beside the cottage in front (16). This narrow road climbs steeply through the forest before levelling out to a viewpoint and picnic area on the right (17). In half a mile (800 m) turn left ⇨ Geirionydd (18). This narrow scenic road twists and turns through the forest for a mile and a half (2.4 km) to a picnic site and toilets on the banks of Llyn Geirionydd (19).

This next stretch is where the navigator comes into his/her own, for there are several gates to be opened and shut. Keep to this road, ignoring turn offs, to a cluster of houses, a chapel and a phone box. Take the sharp left turn ⇨ Trefriw and keep going high above the Conwy valley, glimpses of which can be seen through the trees. Continue to the outskirts of Trefriw over the speed humps to a T-junction (20). Descend steeply down to join the main B5106 in the village. Follow this road for 10 miles (16.1 km) back to Conwy passing the Roman Spa and Dolgarrog (see Link 8 [14 to 17]) Shortly after passing through Ty'n-y-groes is the Groes Inn; this well-known hostelry is reputed to be the first pub in Wales to be licensed in 1573. Approaching Conwy follow the road to the right at the bottom of the hill in Gyffin and then left under the railway bridge, through the town walls, back into the centre.

For detailed heritage, full-colour guides to this historic area see **Welcome to Conwy** and **Welcome to Betws-y-coed**, (available in five languages), and **Welcome to Bangor**, (available in Welsh and English editions; www.carreg-gwalch.com).

1. This is the old coach road from Conwy to Bangor avoiding the very hazardous route round the steep cliffs of Penmaen-bach Point. Down on the right is Pensychnant, a mansion house, now a Nature Conservation Centre. Visitors are welcome to the exhibition, lectures, walks etc. This was the family country house of the well-known Stott family of industrialists in Oldham,.

2. Penmaenmawr: as with so many Welsh villages, this is dominated by a vast quarry – the main suppliers of crushed granite in the UK. There is a useful large clock high in the quarry and visible from the coast road.

   The opening of the expressway by-passed the town, causing the closure of many shops, and it now has a somewhat derelict air. Nevertheless it was once the favourite holiday haunt of William Gladstone, five times Prime Minister in Victorian times.

   On the mountain behind are the remains of a Stone Age axe factory near Graiglwyd; also nearby is the Druid's Circle, one of the best-known Bronze Age stone circles in Wales.

   There is a small museum at No. 4 New York Cottages at the far end of the main street (parking left after the cottage and left again into Masonic Hall car park).

3. Llanfairfechan: the promenade looks out over the wide expanse of Traeth Lafan to Ynys Môn (*Anglesey*) and Ynys Seiriol (*Puffin Island*).

   Beaumaris across the water is a popular holiday town for those interested in sailing and old buildings; the old court house, gaol complete with treadmill and condemned cell, and a delightful Castle are all open to the public, as well as several old hostelries worthy of a visit.

   St Seiriol established a monastery on Puffin Island in the sixth century. The telegraph station, like the puffins, have long gone; the former to advances in communications and the latter to a delicacy when pickled and the depredation of rats!

In Llanfairfechan, those interested in architecture may well wish to see the distinctive estate of houses built by the well-known architects, North and Padmore, in the 1920s. These are approached through the old village which lies across the traffic lights. Just after leaving the village there will be seen on the hillside to the left a plantation of trees in the shape of a cross, a memorial to the Americans who died when their Liberator, 'Bachelor Baby', crashed in 1944.

4. Abergwyngregyn: the road in the village leads up to the grand Aber Falls, where after 0.75 mile (1.2 km) there is a car park and toilets. If one now has the time and energy to walk the 1.5 miles (2.5 km) from the car park along a beautiful valley they will be rewarded with the spectacular sight of the water plunging down 170 feet to the rocks below. The Roman road over the mountains to the Conwy valley starts from here.

Aber has other claims to fame: back down on the eastern side of the village it has recently been proved that Llywelyn had a palace in the grounds of what is now a prominent house, Pen-y-bryn. Legend has it that William De Braose seduced Princess Joan, wife of Llywelyn and daughter of King John, and was hung from a tree in Aber for his treason.

In more modern times the Chester and Holyhead Railway Company installed, in 1871, the world's first water trough between the rails enabling trains to take on water without having to stop on their express journey to Caergybi *(Holyhead)*. The practice was discontinued in 1962 when diesel engines were introduced.

5. Penrhyn Castle: this pseudo-Norman castle was built in the early nineteenth century for the wealthy Pennant family whose fortunes were made from sugar plantations in the West Indies – where slaves would have been used – and, later, slate from their vast quarry at Bethesda. The second Lord Penrhyn was much involved in the infamous three year strike/lock-out in 1900. The family's wealth is obvious in the opulent interior; the grand staircase which took ten years to build; the one ton slate bed made for Queen Victoria (hopefully she slept well in what must surely have been an uncomfortable bed!); the fine furnishings, fabulous paintings and much more. Some might consider this show of wealth obscene knowing its provenance. Nevertheless, the castle (now owned by the National Trust) is well worth visiting. Apart from the castle itself there is a railway museum, a dolls museum, Victorian kitchens and extensive gardens and parkland.

6. Port Penrhyn: developed by the Penrhyn family in 1790 from a small inlet, the harbour could accommodate ships of 300 tons for the export of slates from their massive quarry in Bethesda. The two were connected by a six-mile (9.6 km) narrow gauge tramway in 1801. The mainline railway arrived 50 years later.

7. As a city Bangor has not a great deal to offer. Hemmed in between the rock face of Bangor Mountain and the Menai Strait it is long and narrow. Most of the shops are on a mile (1.6 km) long street, and since it is a university town they tend to cater for the students. The University College opened in 1884 and the present main building dates from 1907. From small beginnings the student population is now well over 7,000 and growing. It is pre-eminent in several fields, particularly marine sciences.

Another important educational establishment is the Normal

Teaching College established in 1858.

St Deiniol founded his Cathedral in 525 AD, pre-dating Canterbury by 70 years and making it the oldest bishopric in Britain. The present building dates from the thirteenth century, though it was destroyed by Owain Glyndŵr in 1402 and extensively restored in the nineteenth century. A special feature is the 'Mostyn Christ', a life-size figure of Christ carved in oak.

Other notable features of the City are its museum; the small theatre attached to the University, and a restored long Victorian pier.

8. Bethesda: in its heyday this rather dismal village, astride the A5, once boasted five chapels, including the one that gave the place its name, and two churches. This was in the days when 2,000 of the menfolk worked in the vast Penrhyn slate quarries across the river. The quarry in total employed 3,000 men who dug a hole a 1,000 feet deep, made up of 21 galleries of varying depth. They also laid 50 miles (80 km) of tramway, to take the slate to the narrow gauge railway which ran down to Port Penrhyn. Each gallery had a 'caban' where meals were eaten, politics discussed, and singing took place.

It was in these 'cabans', no doubt, that the men discussed their grievances in 1900, which led to the most acrimonious, and – at three years – the longest strike in Welsh industrial relations, a field in which the management appears to have been lacking. The quarry never fully recovered and went into decline, along with the town, so that now it provides work for only a handful of men.

Of the two churches, one, St Ann's, lies buried beneath the huge mountain of slate waste, and several of the chapels closed. Apart from that there is now little of interest in the town. Just out of the village a sharp right turn down to a caravan park leads to an impressive road bridge which now ends only in a footpath confronted by a huge waste tip, but just down the path to the right are quite impressive waterfalls.

9. Nant Ffrancon: this wide glacial valley, through which the river Ogwen runs, has the Carneddau range of mountains to the east and the Elidirs to the west. As the valley narrows, the road becomes hemmed in by Pen yr Ole Wen to the left and the Glyderau to the right, all over 3,000 feet. This is serious rock-climbing country.

10. The rather unusual Life Foundation International Course Centre, which caters for those seeking spiritual and physical well-being, is based here. An interesting feature in the forecourt is the 'World Peace Flame' lit from flames brought over from the various continents, and which now burns perpetually in this rather remote part of the UK.

11. Llyn Ogwen: there is a car park at the foot of the lake where the river Ogwen tumbles 70 m down into Nant Ffrancon. There is a half-hour walk from the car park up to the popular Llyn Idwal, a small glacial lake which is a magnet for botanists, geologists and climbers. The Idwal Slabs are a steep wall of rock on which many budding climbers have cut their teeth and the lake is overlooked by Twll Du (*the Devil's Kitchen*), a cleft in the steep rocks. The whole area is a National Nature Reserve with a trail. The Ogwen Valley Mountain Rescue Organisation is based here, as well as the Ogwen Cottage Residential Outdoor Centre.

Further along the lake, at a point known as Milestone Buttress, the sheer rock face overshadows the road. This is such a popular starting point to get on the mountain that, on the day in April 2001 when foot and mouth disease restrictions were lifted, walkers had to queue to get on this well-known rock-climbing buttress.

12. Capel Curig: this village is at the parting of the ways. In 1804 Lord Penrhyn built a road on the western side of the valley terminating in the Capel Curig Inn, 0.5 mile (800 m) down the A4086. Telford, however, favoured the other side of the valley, thus by-passing the inn, with the consequent loss of custom. At that time almost all travellers from England would be heading down to Bangor and very few on the road to Snowdon and Beddgelert, which passed the hotel. Nowadays the Irish traffic uses the A55 expressway and the A5 is relatively quiet with many people now branching off on the A4086 to the heart of Snowdonia. Princess Victoria stayed at the hotel before becoming Queen, and along with other notables, scratched her name on a window pane with her diamond ring, after which the name of the hotel was changed to The Royal. In 1955 the hotel was taken over by the Plas y Brenin Outdoor Pursuits Centre.

Just a little further on is Llynnau Mymbyr, where there is a car park beside the lake with a superb view of the Snowdon Horseshoe range of mountains in the distance. The view is framed on the left by Moel Siabod (2861 ft – 870 m) and on the right by the steep slopes of the Glyderau. At the far end of the lake is Dyffryn Mymbyr, made famous in the book *I Bought a Mountain* by Thomas Firbank.

13. Cobden's Hotel: named after Frank Cobden, a famous cricketer who settled here and died in 1932. The back bar is a popular watering hole for many climbers and walkers.

14. Ty'n-y-coed Hotel: the stagecoach, which stands across the road from this hotel is a replica. The original eighteenth-century one was brought here by the eminent Welsh actor, Emlyn Williams, who starred in the film. *Jamaica Inn*, in which the stagecoach was used.

15. Halfway along this road on the left is the site of a Roman encampment, Caer Llugwy. Coincidently, opposite it on the other side of the river is a present day British army camp.

16. Tŷ Hyll (*the ugly house*) is a well-known feature on the A5. Built in the fifteenth century of massive boulders, it is now the headquarters of the Snowdonia National Park Society, who have restored and refurnished it. Worth a quick visit.

Note: Turning right on the main road before crossing the bridge brings you, after 0.25 mile (400 m), to the famous Rhaeadr Ewynnol (*Swallow Falls*), with hotel and parking.

17. The spectacular views from this picnic site look out over the wooded hills around Betws-y-coed, itself hidden in the valley below. Looking to the left in the distance are the Denbigh Moors, whilst just to the right, in the far distance, can just be seen the Cader Idris range.

18. Before taking this turning carry on for 200 m to the site of the old Cyffty lead mines of the 1850s. The remains have been preserved, and an information board gives details of the numerous other lead and zinc mines in the area, all now abandoned. Return to the Geirionydd turning.

19. Llyn Geirionydd: one of the many attractive lakes in this area, with a pleasant walk round – though at one point, on the far side, beware of the exposed tree roots. There is also a forest trail.

At the far end of the lake, on a mound above the outlet, is a prominent memorial to mark the alleged birthplace of Taliesin, chief bard, in the sixth century.

20. If time permits, a left turn follows a narrow road alongside the river Crafnant for two miles to the very scenic Llyn Crafnant. There is a car park and toilets in the forest on the right just before the lake. A monument tells of the benefactor, Richard James, who gave the lake to the people of Llanrwst in 1896. Again there is a pleasant and level walk around the lake and partway round there is a café from where rowing boats can be hired. As there is no vehicular way out of the valley it is necessary to return back down to the village of Trefriw.

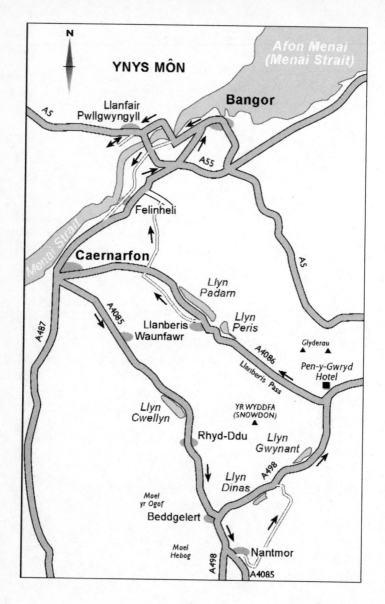

Link 10

Bangor – Caernarfon – Bangor

Distance: 60 miles (97 kilometers)
Time: 4 hours plus stops

Description

This journey commences with a short detour across the water onto
Ynys Môn (*Anglesey*) over two historic bridges and a visit to that
famous village with the long name:
Llanfairpwllgwyngyllgogerychwyrndrobwllantysiliogogogoch. Then
on to the historic town of Caernarfon. Next the route climbs right
into the heart of Eryri (*Snowdonia*) with a circuit of Yr Wyddfa
(*Snowdon*) itself. Returning via the vast slate quarries and
attractions of Llanberis.

Perhaps the best focal point in Bangor is the railway station. From
here proceed down the road in front, the A5122 (formerly the A5),
with the University buildings on the left and, at the far end, where the
main road bends round to the right, take the narrow street ahead
which leads to the pier (1). Follow the narrow one-way road up the hill
to the left, initially through trees but later opening out with a viewpoint
on the right overlooking the Menai Strait. The building on the left is
the Normal Teacher Training College. On joining the main road turn
right and in just over a mile (1.6 km) take the second exit at the
roundabout by the Antelope Inn to cross the Menai Suspension
Bridge (2) onto Ynys Môn (*Anglesey*). At the far side of the bridge go
ahead at the first roundabout and the first exit at the second ⇨
Caergybi *(Holyhead)*; the town of Porthaethwy *(Menai Bridge)* (3) is
to the right. In just under a mile (1.6 km) there is a lay-by on the left

giving a panoramic view across the Strait (4). Pass under the expressway and continue into the village of Llanfair Pwllgwyngyll (5).

Turn at the James Pringle outlet to return from the village passing under the expressway again but this time immediately turn right to join the slip road onto the Britannia Bridge (6). After crossing the bridge take the next exit and at the roundabout at the bottom take the third exit to pass under the expressway (to view the underside of the bridge take the first exit and then the secondary road on the left; the metalled road giving way to a rough lane leading down to the water's edge) to another roundabout, taking the first exit ➪ Caernarfon. The high stone wall on the right marks the boundary of the Faenol Estate (7). At the roundabout at the bottom of the hill take the third exit ➪ Y Felinheli (*Port Dinorwig*) (8) and follow the estate wall round into the village. The short road down to the harbour is opposite Tŷ Hanner Ffordd (*the halfway house*), but carry on to the far end of the village, and just after the pedestrian crossing take the narrow, rather quaint, steep street on the right which leads down to the sea front. There is parking here with a fine view across the Strait. a pub, and toilets. Follow the terrace of houses along the front to the boatyard, where passing through, the road rises steeply to rejoin the main road, with a church in front. Turn right and continue for 1.25 miles (2 km) to the roundabout; take the third exit ➪ Caernarfon (9); go straight ahead at the next roundabout, by the entrance to Morrison's supermarket, and then take the third exit. This street leads into Y Maes (*the square*); go round to the far side and down, between the castle and the statue of Lloyd George, to the Slate Quay and car park.

Return journey

Leave the harbour by the road round the base of this massive castle, past the Courts on the left, and take the one-way street on the left opposite the entrance to the castle, Castle Street. After passing through the town walls turn right and then left at the mini-roundabout. Follow this road up to the roundabout by Morrison's again, and this time take the third exit onto the town centre by-pass. At the far end follow the road round to the left and go straight ahead up the A4085 (beware of traffic coming up on the left and wanting to cross to the far side lane). At the top of the rise look out on the left for Segontium Roman Fort (10). The entrance is not all that easy to spot and the small museum looks, at first glance, like a private house, but it is signposted and for anyone interested in archaeology it is a must.

Keep to the A4085, going straight ahead at the next roundabout and in a couple of miles (3.2 km) pass through the village of Waunfawr (11). Keep on and shortly pass through the hamlet of Betws Garmon (12) to arrive on the banks of Llyn Cwellyn, on the far side of which, the sheer, tree-covered slopes of Mynydd Mawr fall into the water. Halfway along the lake, which supplies water to Caernarfon, there is a car park on the right and opposite, the Snowdon Ranger Youth Hostel (13).

The next hamlet is Rhyd-ddu (14) where there is excellent parking and toilets, on the left, by the current terminus of the Welsh Highland Railway. A little further on down the A4085, with Llyn y Gadair and the Beddgelert Forest (15) on the right, the road continues down hill into the village of Beddgelert (16). Parking is a little restricted during the height of the season but turning right over the bridge and following the road round there is a car park in on the right just before the Goat Hotel.

Leaving the village going south, on the A498, the road follows the banks of the river Glaslyn, dominated on the right by the impressive 2,600 ft (782 m) of Moel Hebog. This is the beautiful Pass of Aberglaslyn, popular with calendar and chocolate box makers! The river was navigable up to Pont Aberglaslyn until William Madocks built his embankment at Porthmadog in the early 1800s to reclaim thousands of acres of land.

Turn left over the bridge on the A4085 and very shortly there is a car park and toilets on the left in the hamlet of Nantmor (17). Leave the main road, and take the minor road on the left through the houses. This attractive road twists and turns, with some short sharp hills until after a mile (1.6 km) it comes to a T-junction by a house called Bwlchgwernog. Turn left into what is now the Nanmor valley and follow closely the banks of the river through woods with picnic areas, until after 3 miles (4.8 km) of fairly gentle climbing it emerges into open countryside, with views across the valley on the right to a range of mountains including Cnicht 2,265 ft (689 m), Moel Druman 2,152 ft (676 m) and Ysgafell Wen 2,299 ft (660 m) and in the opposite direction, the Snowdon Horsehoe range.

At the crest of the hill there is a sharp left turn and the road begins to drop down eventually to cross the river Glaslyn onto the A498. Turn right and almost immediately there is a car park and toilets on the right. This is the start of the Watkin Path up Yr Wyddfa (*Snowdon*) (18). The road now starts its steady climb, initially along the shores of Llyn Gwynant and then more steeply to where there are two viewpoints on the left, the higher one giving perhaps the better view of Snowdon (19). (There is frequently a welcome ice cream van here in the season.)

Continue to the top of the hill and take the road on the left, the A4086, by the Penygwryd Hotel (20). The road climbs up to the Pass of Llanberis at Pen-y-pass (21). There is limited parking here and those wishing to stop a while, perhaps to climb Snowdon, would be well advised (particularly in high season) to get here either very early or better still take one of the Sherpa buses which ply from various points in the Park.

The road down from the pass follows the river Nant Peris, with the flank of Snowdon on the south side and the sheer rock faces of the Glyderau and Y Garn to the north. These rock faces are popular, and at weekends and in season they are crawling with climbers testing their skill. The lay-by on the left is usually full of motorists watching in awe of this seemingly dangerous pastime.

Halfway down the hill just after the bridge, Pont y Gromlech, a large boulder on the right is reputed to have been the abode of an old woman named Hetty while she looked after her sheep and goats. Popular outcry prevented its removal by the authorities in a road-widening scheme! At the foot of the hill is the hamlet of Nant Peris, a centre for campers and climbers, where the only pub is full of these outdoor types in the evening.

The road now follows the shores of Llyn Peris (22), bending to avoid Castell Dolbadarn (23) before entering the village of Llanberis (24). There is parking across the road from the Snowdon Mountain Railway terminus, near the Welsh Slate Museum to the right, and limited space overlooking the lake on the village centre by-pass.

Take the main street rather than the by-pass and halfway along go up Goodman Street on the left (opposite Pete's Café). After leaving the built-up area the road begins to climb through woods. Breaking out from the trees are the spoil heaps of the vast Glyn Rhonwy slate quarry (25) and it is interesting to just stop at the side of the road to get out and look down into the actual quarry. The road climbs more steeply through a series of sharp bends becoming narrow – very narrow in places – unfenced, and with a poor surface, requiring care.

At the top the views are stunning, so find a spot to park and get out. Looking back, down to the left Llanberis and Llyn Padarn, behind which rise the much quarried foothills of Elidir Fawr 3,030 ft (930 m), whilst to the right there is the 'V' of the Llanberis Pass, with the Glyderau (Fach and Fawr), both over 3,000 ft (900 m) on the north side of the Pass, and Crib Goch and Yr Wyddfa, again well over 3,000 ft (900 m) on the south side.

Over the cattle grid the road begins to drop down to Bryn Bras Castle (26) passing a reservoir and caravan site on the left and then the outbuildings of the castle itself. Soon, turn right at the X-roads and ahead at the next X-roads to drop down to Pont Rhythallt over the river Rhythallt – the outflow of Llyn Padarn. Keep straight ahead up the narrower road at the next X-roads and follow this pleasant road for a couple of miles (3.2 km), ignoring those coming in from the right and left, as it dips down into valleys and finally joins the main B4366 to turn right by the Gors Bach inn. Take the next minor road on the left ⇨ Seion, before joining the main B4547 after 2 miles (3.2 km). Turn left and drop down through the forest to join the A487(T). Turn right and at the roundabout take the second exit ⇨ Bangor A4087. Follow this road straight into the city and, after passing under the railway bridge, turn immediately left on the one-way system keeping to the left-hand lane back to the railway station.

For detailed heritage, full-colour guides to this historic area see **Welcome to Caernarfon** and **Welcome to Llanberis**, (available in five languages), and **Welcome to Bangor** and **Welcome to Llanfairpwll**, (available in Welsh and English editions; www.carreg-gwalch.com).

1. Bangor's Victorian pier, like most in the country, had fallen into disrepair before being rescued and has now been restored to its former glory. It appears to stretch all the way to Ynys Môn but in fact is just over half way across Menai Strait. Nevertheless a walk along it is rewarded by fine views of the strait in both directions.

2. Until Thomas Telford built this famous bridge in 1826, as part of his route from London to Holyhead, and then by ferry on to Dublin, Anglesey was a true island with access only by a hazardous ferry crossing. The bridge is a larger version of the one he built to cross the Conwy estuary. It has a central span of 579 ft (176 m) and, to comply with requirements from the Admiralty to permit the passage of sailing ships, the carriageway is 100 ft (30.5 m) above high water. Although built to take horse drawn vehicles, 150 years later it is still carrying contemporary traffic. The only modification carried out during this period has been the replacement of the original wrought iron chain links with steel in the 1930s, and it will no doubt serve for many more years to come.

3. The town of Porthaethwy *(Menai Bridge)* grew as a result of the bridge, and is now a thriving community. The little church of St Tysilio on Church Island warrants inspection. It is linked to the town by a causeway and a promenade that was built during the First World War by Belgian refugees.

4. The Strait stretches for 18 miles (30 km) from Ynys Seiriol *(Puffin Island)* in the north east to Abermenai in the south west. Great care has to be taken navigating the Strait. There are numerous sand banks at low tide, and the stretch of water between the two bridges, known as The Swellies, has strong tidal currents. There are several small islands, the chief of which is Ynys Gored Goch, formerly the home of a fisherman who maintained a weir and fish trap. The island is now a holiday retreat.

In 1941 the 92-gun warship, *HMS Conway* (formerly *HMS Nile*) on loan from the Admiralty as a training ship, was moved from Liverpool to a mooring by Bangor pier for safety reasons. In 1949 she was moved to a new mooring near Plas Newydd, where a shore base was also established. In 1953, whilst being towed to Liverpool for a refit, she came to grief in The Swellies and was stranded near the Suspension Bridge until, three years later, she caught fire and was destroyed.

The view from this lay-by is stunning. In front, across the Strait, the backdrop of the mountains of Snowdonia; to the right, Pont Britannia; to the left the Menai Suspension Bridge, and down below the islets and fast-moving currents of The Swellies.

5. The true name of this village is Llanfair Pwllgwyngyll, but is more famously known as having the longest name of any village. In Victorian times, with an eye to tourism, the local tailor added many more letters so that it became Llanfairpwllgwyngyllgogerych-wyrndrobwllantysiliogogogoch, which, translated, means *'St Mary's Church in the hollow of the white hazel near the rapid whirlpool of Llantysilio near the red cave'*. The railway company, to cash in on this, issued tickets with the full name. The station is now closed but tickets can still be obtained from James Pringle retail outlet!

In fact the village has no need for its frankly ridiculous, name, for it has many other attractions of interest to the tourist. On entering the village will be seen, on the right, the tall column erected by the villagers as a tribute to the 1st Marquess of Anglesey who, as Wellington's aide at Waterloo, lost a leg in battle and is attributed with making the (possibly apocryphal) remark 'By God sir, I've lost my leg' to which Wellington is purported to have replied 'By God, so you have'. The column in 90 ft (27.4 m) high and those with sufficient stamina, climbing the 115 steps will be rewarded with fine views.

Plas Newydd, the Angleseys' family seat, is a mile down the road to the left and, apart from its setting, the fine house, now owned by the National Trust is noted for the large mural by Rex Whistler in the dining room, and a Waterloo museum, which includes the first Marquess's artificial leg.

In the angle between the two roads at the turnoff to Plas Newydd is one of Telford's little tollhouses listing the various charges for using the turnpike road. Behind it is the building where the first Women's Institute in Britain met, modelled on that in Canada. On the opposite side of the road from the Column there is a memorial in the churchyard to those who died during the construction of Pont Britannia. A little further down on the foreshore is a statue of Nelson erected after the Battle of Trafalgar.

6. In 1850 Robert S. Stephenson completed his railway crossing of the Menai Strait, using the same tubular steel construction as his smaller Conwy crossing. It had a span of 450 feet (137 m) and sufficient height to allow passage of sailing ships. London was now linked to Holyhead, and in that year *The Irish Mail* left London at 7.30 am and arrived in Holyhead at 2.00 pm – a vast improvement on the previous stagecoaches which took days to complete the journey.

In 1970 some children searching for bats accidentally set fire to the wooden lining and the bridge was virtually destroyed, turning the clock back to pre-1850 days when the Menai Suspension Bridge provided the only link. It was several years before the rail link was to be restored and by that time a second road crossing was needed. The new bridge is a single arch span with the road running above the railway, utilising the original massive stone pillars. Down below the bridge, at the mainland end, the 25 ft x 12 ft (3.28 m x 3.7 m) high, stone lions each weighing 30 tons still guard the railway line, as Stephenson intended. Also to be seen there is a section of the original tubular steel bridge showing its construction.

7. Faenol Estate: the family fortunes of the Assheton-Smiths, whose estate lies behind this high stone wall, were hewn from the mountainside in Llanberis where the vast Dinorwig slate quarry in its heyday employed 2,500 men with an annual output of over 87,000 tons. The park is not generally open to the public, but the present incumbent, Sir Michael Duff, opens it every August Bank Holiday weekend for Bryn Terfel, the famous opera singer, who organises a big outdoor concert. Part of the estate has been made into an enterprise park, and a section down by the Strait belongs to the National Trust. The family owned large tracts of Eryri (*Snowdonia*), including Yr Wyddfa (*Snowdon*) itself, which they sold to the National Trust in 1998.

8. Y Felinheli (*Port Dinorwig*): this small creek on the banks of the Strait was developed by the Assheton-Smiths to handle the slates from their quarry in Llanberis from where a 7-mile (11 km) narrow gauge railway was built in 1840. The slates have gone and the little harbour is now filled with pleasure boats. Until the 1940s a ferry plied from here to Moel-y-don on the other side. The prominent tall-spired church in the field opposite is Llanedwen and appears rather large for what must surely be a small congregation. A gravestone in the churchyard bears the following inscription:

'Stop a foot and cast an eye
As you are now so once was I.
As I am now so must you be,
Prepare yourself to follow me.'

9. Caernarfon: there is not a great deal of interest in this historic town apart, of course, from its magnificent castle built by Edward I between 1283 and 1327 to subjugate the Welsh. The narrow streets within the town walls and the harbour are full of character. For further information see Link 1 (1).

10. Segontium: this important Roman Fort was established here in 77 AD by Agricola. Designed to accommodate 1,000 men, the layout of the fort, which was excavated in the 1920s, is clearly visible. There is an interesting small museum to which admission is free.

11. Waunfawr: this rather uninspiring village's claim to fame is that, in 1914, Marconi established, above the village, what was the first commercial transmitting station for radio signals to America. The 300 Kw transmitter broadcast on a wavelength of 10,000 metres. In 1918 William Morris Hughes, Welsh Prime Minister of Australia, sent the first message in Morse code to his country. The world's first picture was sent by radio from here – a photograph of the Derby winner in 1927. So that signals could be received back from America a reciprocal station was established 70 miles down the coast, at Tywyn (see Link 5 [4]). The station closed down in 1939 and little remains of its existence.

12. Betws Garmon: this hamlet, straddling the A4085, has a fine three-arched bridge built in the eighteenth century by a well-known local man, Harry Parry. There is also a pretty little nineteenth-century church.

13. John Morton, one of the earliest guides in the 1800s, referred to himself as The Snowdon Ranger and this, one of the seven established paths up Snowdon, is known by that name. The other routes are the Rhyd-ddu Path, the Watkin Path, the Miners' Track, the Pyg Track, the Crib Goch route, and the Llanberis Path. His house became a hotel and is now a Youth Hostel. There is parking opposite.

14. One of the best routes up Snowdon, the Rhyd-ddu Path starts from the car park here. This is one of the stops on the Welsh Highland Railway to Porthmadog.

This is the birthplace of T. H. Parry-Williams a well-known man of letters.

15. Beddgelert Forest: this Forest Park was established in 1937. There are many trails with picnic and camping areas. Picturesque little Llyn Llywelyn hidden in the centre is an attractive spot. At the far south western end of the forest is Moel yr Ogof, a 2,300 ft (655 m) peak with a cave *(ogof)* where Owain Glyndŵr hid from English forces after his long campaign for Welsh independence.

16. Beddgelert: although always popular with early travellers the village really took off at the beginning of the nineteenth century when David Pritchard, landlord of the Goat Hotel, in order to drum up business, started the legend of 'Gelert'. The faithful hound, the legend has it, was killed by his master on the mistaken assumption that it had killed his child, whereas it had in fact protected the child from a wolf. The 'grave of Gelert' is in the field a short walk down the river and is still a big tourist attraction.

Older readers will remember the Rupert Bear annuals and cartoons in the *Daily Express*. Alfred Bestall, who wrote and illustrated these for decades from 1935, maintained a holiday cottage, later his home, just outside the village. He died in 1986 and is buried in Penrhyndeudraeth.

In 1949 the Prince Llywelyn Hotel was hit by a 1¾ lb (875 grms) meteorite which is on display.

There are plenty of hotels, cafes and shops, including an award-winning ice cream parlour. At the height of the season and at weekends the village understandably gets very busy, for it is a very popular walking centre.

17. Nantmor: from the car park a path leads, under the trackbed of the old Welsh Highland Railway, into Cwm Bychan where the lower workings of the copper mines further up the valley, on Mynydd Sygyn, can be seen. The circular foundation, called buddles, were used to separate the ore which was brought down the Cwm by aerial ropeway – at that time an innovation, since most mines and quarries used trucks on inclines. The mines do not appear to have been successful.

Another path going to the left from behind the toilets leads to one of the most photographed views in Snowdonia – the Aberglaslyn Pass.

18. This is Bethania Bridge in the Gwynant valley, with its small car park and toilets. Across the road is the start of the ever-popular Watkin Path up Yr Wyddfa (*Snowdon*), named after Sir Edward Watkins who, in 1892, owned the land and built a holiday bungalow to accommodate his many visitors. This is the longest route to the summit, but is fairly easy going until the last few hundred feet where it becomes something of a scramble.

At the lower end of the path there are attractive falls on the river Cwm Llan.

The most notable event occurred in 1892 when William Gladstone, aged 84, gave a speech part-way up the path attended by a vast crowd, including Lloyd George. A tablet on the rock from which he spoke commemorates the event.

A couple of miles (3.2 km) back down the Gwynant valley,

beyond Llyn Dinas, but not on our route, is a prominent hill, Dinas Emrys, featured in Welsh folklore as recorded in *The Mabinogion*. Originally an Iron Age and Roman fort, then a Welsh castle, it is associated with King Arthur and Vortigern. It is said that two dragons – one red, one white – fought here. The former won, hence the national flag.

19. This is a truly stunning viewpoint. Ranged in front are the mountains of the Snowdon Horseshoe; following round from the right, Crib Goch 3,023 ft (923 m), Garnedd Ugain 3,495 ft (1,065 m), Yr Wyddfa (*Snowdon*) 3,560 ft (1,085 m), and Lliwedd 2,947 ft (898 m). The view is somewhat marred by the twin pipes taking water from Llyn Llydaw, in the shadow of Yr Wyddfa, down Cwm Dyli to the hydro-electric station in the valley below – built in 1903 and still in use. The view down the valley over Llyn Gwynant and Llyn Dinas ends with the impressive Moel Hebog 2,566 ft (782 m). In the distance up to the right, are the mountains of Tryfan and the Glyderau, all over 3,000 ft (900 m).

20. Famed the world over by climbers, the Penygwryd Hotel has played host to many of the leading names in the climbing fraternity since it was built in the early 1800s, as well as many distinguished politicians and men of letters. The members of the 1953 successful Everest expedition established their training headquarters here, and before leaving, signed their names on the ceiling, now preserved. Across the road is the site of a Roman camp.

21. This is the starting point of the three of the most popular routes up Snowdon since there are only 2,000 ft (610m) left to climb! The Miners' Track, so called after the miners who toiled in the copper mines above and who might well have walked up from Llanberis, follows the shores of Llyn Teyrn, Llyn Llydaw and Llyn Glaslyn. The Pyg Track is possibly named after Bwlch y Moch ('pass of the pigs'). Both paths are fairly easy until the last steep climb to the summit. The Grib Goch route is for the more agile without a fear of heights. The National Trust bought the mountain largely with a million pound donation from the Welsh actor Anthony Hopkins. At the car park there is a café, toilets and information point. Across the road is the Pen-y-pass Youth Hostel, formerly the Gorphwysfa Hotel – another firm favourite with the climbers of the time. Chief among these was Geoffrey Winthrop Young, a mountaineer and poet, who organised the famous Easter parties here. He died, aged 82, in 1958.

22. Nant Peris: this tiny hamlet has nothing to commend it except that it is the starting point for many walks in the area and is close to the rock faces of Elidir Fawr and Y Garn favoured by the climbers. There is a pub, a simple church, and a car park from where the 'Sherpa' bus service operates.

23. Castell Dolbadarn: guarding the entrance to the Llanberis Pass, this castle was built by Llywelyn Fawr (*the Great*) in the thirteenth century. The last Prince Llywelyn held his brother, Owain Goch, captive here for twenty years. Its dramatic situation has made it a favourite with artists, including Turner.

24. Llanberis: there is so much to see and do here that it warrants at least a full day. First, the Snowdon Mountain Railway, the only rack and pinion railway in Britain, opened in 1896, starts from here and terminates within 66 ft of the summit - at what was described by Charles of Windsor as 'the highest slum in the country'! The buildings, a café and station etc., were designed by Clough Williams-Ellis of Portmeirion fame and, whatever Charles may have thought, and few would disagree with him, they were a considerable improvement on the collection of huts that existed prior to the late 1920s. The building has now been demolished and a more appropriate edifice is being erected in its place.

According to legend King Arthur slew the giant Rhita and his body is buried beneath the summit – hence the name Yr Wyddfa, meaning 'burial cairn'. Arthur himself is said to have been mortally wounded and is buried beneath a cairn called Carnedd Arthur. His knights lie asleep in a nearby cave awaiting his resurrection. On a clear day the Wicklow hills in Ireland, the Isle of Man and the Lake District mountains are visible. The railway was officially opened on Easter Monday 1896 – and was closed on the same day for twelve months, following an accident on the inaugural journey which resulted in one fatality. Many people walk up alongside the track as a relatively easy, though longer, path to the summit.

Looking across Llyn Peris it is possible to fully appreciate the extent to which quarrying was carried out in this area. This, the Dinorwig quarry, closed in 1969 but in its heyday, 2,500 men hacked away the side of Elidir Fawr to produce an annual output of nearly 90,000 tons of slate. (The other side of the mountain was being attacked by the Penrhyn quarry.)

The Electric Mountain Visitor Centre explains, with interactive displays, how the power of water is used to produce electricity. This is the starting point for tours to see the power station deep within the mountain. The main feature is the vast cavern, 587 ft (180 m) long x 80 ft (24.4 m) wide x 200 ft (61 m) high which houses the turbines and generators. During off peak periods water is pumped up from Llyn Peris to Marchlyn Mawr reservoir high in the mountain to be released at times of peak demand to power the turbines and generators. The advantage of this scheme is that it can be brought on-load in a matter of minutes.

The Museum and Galleries of Wales has a display of paintings here on all aspects of Snowdonia. Just the other side of Llyn Padarn is the Quarry Hospital Visitor Centre which is exactly as it was when the quarry was working, complete with gruesome surgical instruments and mortuary!

The Welsh Slate Museum next door is based on the quarry workshops and has much of the original equipment, driven by a huge water wheel. There is a restored group of quarrymen's cottages, and demonstrations are given on the production of slates. The finished product was taken by rail to the harbour of Felinheli and part of this line now runs down the north side of Llyn Padarn hauled by original locomotives; there is a halt and picnic site half way along. The lake is part of Parc Gwledig Padarn (Padarn Country Park) and there are walks, nature trails and boating on the lake.

25. The vast Glyn Rhonwy quarry was used during the war as a huge bomb storage complex, and as a sideline women were employed to load machine gun ammunition belts. Wages at that time were £5 per week with an addition of 5/- (25p) danger money. After the war the problem was the disposal of remaining bombs, both high explosive and incendiary. The site was not declared safe until 1975.

26. Bryn Bras Castle: as castles go this one is fairly modern, having been built in 1830. Some rooms are open to the public and the 30-acre (12 hectare) garden is itself worth a visit. The road to the right of the castle leads to the little community of Cwm-y-glo where, in 1869, two carts each carrying a ton of the very unstable nitro-glycerine exploded, killing five people and causing considerable damage.

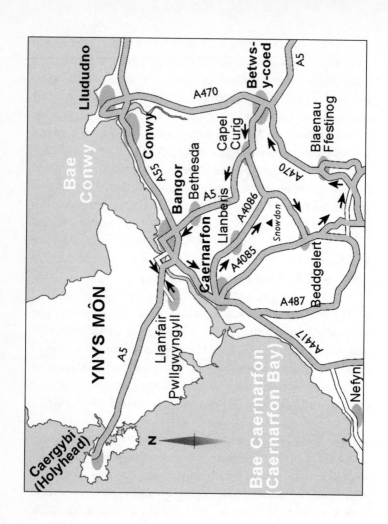

170

Appendix 1

For those who have neither time, nor inclination for a more detailed exploration of the Snowdonia National Park here are two journeys that give an overview of the area. The first covers the north part of Snowdonia based on Snowdon itself, and the second, based on Cader Idris, covers the southern area. Each route can be accomplished in a day and to this end the minor roads have been omitted.

1. Northern Snowdonia National Park

Description
Starting from the Slate Quay at Caernarfon follow the road round the base of this massive castle, started by Edward I in 1283 and only finished by his son in 1327. This one-way street leads back into Y Maes (the main square) but before then take the street on the left opposite the castle entrance. At the bottom after passing through the remains of the town walls, turn right and then at the mini-roundabout turn left. Follow this road up to the roundabout by Morrison's supermarket and take the third exit onto the town centre by-pass. Almost immediately take the slip road down to the roundabout underneath and leave by the first exit ⇨ Llanberis, the A4086, and keep to this road at the next roundabout, leaving by the second exit.

In a couple of miles (3.2 km) the road crosses to the other bank of the river Seiont at Pont-rug. In a mile and a half (2.4 km) pass through the quarry workers' village of Llanrug and in a similar distance the hamlet of Cwm-y-glo, now by-passed but where, in 1869, two carts carrying the very unstable nitro-glycerine for the quarries exploded, killing five and injuring many more as well as doing considerable damage. This is the point where slates from the huge quarries and copper mines of Llanberis were transferred from the boats that had brought them down Llyn Padarn to carts for onward transmission to Caernarfon before a tramway was built to Y Felinheli (*Port Dinorwig*) in 1824 and the standard gauge railway which arrived in 1869.

The road continues along the bank of Llyn Padarn into Llanberis. The numerous attractions of the Padarn Country Park include: the start of the Snowdon Mountain Railway; the Welsh Slate Museum, a branch of the Museums and Galleries of Wales; the Dinorwig Hydro-Electric Pumped Storage Station, buried in a huge cavern deep inside the mountain; and many others including the Llanberis Lake Railway which runs for 2.5 miles (4 km) on the other side of the lake. There is a Visitor Centre at the Quarry Hospital with a large car park in front. The main street has the usual shops, cafes and hotels. The Royal Victoria Hotel in front on leaving the village, was built in 1832 in the hope of a visit from the future Queen Victoria. She never came, but the hotel became the leading place to stay in Snowdonia. Dolbadarn Castle on the left behind the hotel stands guard at the entrance to the Llanberis Pass. It was built by Llywelyn Fawr (*the Great*) in the thirteenth century and is reputed to be the place where Prince Llywelyn incarcerated his brother for twenty years! The road runs alongside Llyn Peris from where water is pumped, during the night, up to Marchlyn Mawr high above, to be released, during times of high demand, to drive the generators deep inside the mountain. From here it is possible to appreciate just how big the quarry was – it closed in 1969. In its heyday it employed over 2,500 men who between them produced over 80,000 tons per annum.

The road now starts its long climb up to Pen-y-pass, with, on the left, the sheer rock faces of y Garn and the Glyderau – Glyder Fawr and Glyder Fach. A close inspection of these rocks will show that they are usually swarming with climbers, whilst onlookers parked on the opposite side of the road hold their breath as the climbers appear to do the impossible. On the right of the road across the river Nant Peris lie the slopes of Yr Wyddfa (Snowdon). The top of the Pass is the start of three of the accepted routes up Yr Wyddfa – the Miners' Track, the Pyg Track and the more hazardous Crib Goch route. There are a café, and toilets, etc., but parking is particularly difficult. Across the road is the Pen-y-pass Youth Hostel which started out as the Gorphwysfa Hotel and which became famous among climbers, including the notable Geoffrey Winthrop Young, poet and mountaineer.

The Penygwryd Hotel at the foot of the Pass is an even more famous hostelry with the international climbing fraternity. It was here that the 1953 successful Everest expedition were based for their training schedule. Before leaving they all signed their names on the ceiling of the bar – unfortunately some idiots have scrawled over this historic exhibit and it has had to be covered to prevent further damage.

Turn right here to go down the Gwynant valley. Halfway down there is a lay-by on the right with a magnificent view of the Snowdon Horseshoe – from the right, Crib Goch, Garnedd Ugain, Yr Wyddfa and Lliwedd. Unfortunately the view in front is marred by the twin pipelines that carry water down from Llyn Llydaw, in the shadow of Yr Wyddfa, to the Cwm Dyli hydro-electric station in the valley. It was one of the first such stations in Wales having been built in 1906 and is still operational.

Continuing down this beautiful valley, the first lake is Llyn Gwynant, perhaps one of the most scenic. A mile (1.6 km) beyond the bottom of the lake, a lay-by and toilets on the left is the starting point for one of the popular routes up Snowdon – the Watkin Path, from where, in 1892, William Ewart Gladstone, at the age of 84, made a significant speech. A plaque on the rock, 2 miles (3.2 km) up the path, from where he spoke commemorates the event.

Next is Llyn Dinas, another pretty lake, at the foot of which is a prominent mound, Dinas Emrys, important in Welsh folklore for its Arthurian connection and the place where the red dragon beat the white one to become the Welsh symbol.

A further mile (1.6 km) brings us to Beddgelert, the attractive village, famous perhaps for the legend of the hound that was killed by his master in the mistaken belief that it had killed his child – whereas it had in fact been protecting the baby from a wolf. The site of the grave is by the river, but it is now thought that the whole story was part of a publicity campaign, by the landlord of the Goat Inn!

The village is a very popular centre for the many walks in the area and is well supplied with hotels, cafes and shops etc.

Continuing down the river with the bulk of Moel Hebog up to the right, we come to Pont Aberglaslyn, with one of those picture-postcard views back up the Pass. Before the embankment was built at Porthmadog, the river was tidal up to this point.

Turn left over the bridge, on the A4085, where there is a car park and toilets. Keep to this road for 3 miles (4.8 km) and at the staggered X-road in the hamlet of Garreg turn left on the B4410 ⇨ Rhyd. Keep to this pretty narrow road for 4 miles (6.4 km) passing through the few houses that are Rhyd and later under the Ffestiniog Railway at Tan-y-bwlch station to come to lovely Llyn Mair where there is roadside parking with a picnic area by the lake. Continue along the lake to drop down to join the A487 by the Oakley Arms Hotel and turn left. Up to the right is Plas Tan y Bwlch – now the Snowdonia National Park Study Centre but formerly the home of William Oakley, one of the Blaenau Ffestiniog slate barons.

Crossing the river Dwyryd keep to the left and then take the next road on the left, the A496 ⇨ Ffestiniog to follow the beautiful Vale of Ffestiniog as far as the town of Blaenau Ffestiniog (not to be confused with Ffestiniog). On the left is Tanygrisiau Reservoir from where water is pumped up to Llyn Stwlan high above to be released to drive the generators during times of high demand. There is a café.

The town was based entirely on slate, and its industrial past is there for all to see from the spoil heaps that tower over the place and come right down to the road. Blaenau Ffestiniog is now trying to re-invent itself as a tourist centre. At one time it had a population of over 11,000. During the war the nation's art treasures were hidden deep inside the Manod Quarry. The Ffestiniog Railway shares a station with the standard gauge railway that runs down the Lledr and Conwy valleys to Llandudno. At the roundabout follow the A470 ⇨ Betws-y-coed: this is the main north to south Wales trunk road.

On the right on leaving the town are the Llechwedd Slate Caverns, now an award-winning tourist attraction with tours of the caverns deep beneath the mountain and a replica miners' village complete with pub, and of course the usual souvenir shop.

The road now climbs steeply up to the Crimea Pass, thought to have been named after a pub of that name which stood here during the Crimea War. It would have been well patronised by the workers digging the 2 mile (3.2 km) railway tunnel under Moel Druman!

The impressive castle at the entrance to the village of Dolwyddelan was built in the twelfth century by the Welsh and Llywelyn Fawr (*the Great*) was born here in 1173; it fell to the English in 1283 but was reoccupied by the Welsh in the fifteenth century. There is a tiny church of some interest. Follow the road for just under 6 miles (9.6 km) until it joins the A5 and turn left to

175

follow it round over the Waterloo Bridge and enter Betws-y-coed. The village is always busy, for it is a centre for many walks and places of interest in the area. There is a car park by the station where, apart from the main valley line trains there are cafes, shops and a model railway exhibition in the old station buildings. The main street has many cafes, shops and B&Bs.

Follow the main road through and out of the village. In a couple of miles (3.2 km) are the Swallow Falls, a tourist attraction with a hotel and car park opposite. There is a good picnic area on the left just before the road crosses the river Llugwy. In front is Tŷ Hyll (the ugly house), now the Snowdonia Society headquarters. Follow this historic road for the next 17 miles (27 km) into Bangor. This road, the A5, was built by Thomas Telford between 1815 and 1829, at a cost of £1,000 per mile, to improve communications between London and Dublin. This feat of engineering, which included a crossing of the Menai Strait, is still much as he built it, with relatively minor alterations to improve safety. It has been largely superseded by the A55 expressway, which now carries the bulk of commercial traffic. The A5 is a much more pleasant road to drive on.

The stagecoach which stands across the road from the Ty'n-y-coed Hotel is a replica of the original which had been used in the film 'Jamaica Inn'.

The village of Capel Curig lies in a truly magnificent situation surrounded by mountains: Moel Siabod to the south, Snowdon and the Glyderau and Tryfan in front and the Carneddau to the north. The road to the left, the A4086, leads down the Gwynant Valley to Beddgelert and a little way along is Plas y Brenin, formerly the Royal Hotel, now an Outdoor Pursuit Centre, beyond which is an often-photographed, fine view across Llynau Mymbyr, of Snowdon. At the far end of the lake is Dyffryn Mymbyr, the farm featured in the book, *I bought a mountain* by Thomas Firbank.

Continuing down the A5, after 5 miles (8 km) it drops down to Llyn Ogwen at the far end of which there is a car park. This is a Mecca for climbers with Llyn Idwal hidden up to the left and the famous Idwal Slabs, where many young climbers have cut their teeth. There is a short walk and nature trail up to the lake and another to view the Ogwen Falls.

Now follows a 4 mile (6.4 km) straight run down Nant Ffrancon to Bethesda. This quarry village was named after one of the five chapels and two churches that it boasted in the eighteenth and nineteenth centuries when the Penrhyn slate quarry, on the other side of the valley, employed more than 2,000 workers. It is the deepest slate quarry in the world with a depth of 1,000 feet (300 m), and the vast spoil heaps are a blot on the landscape. Although the quarry is still working, the workforce can now be numbered in hundreds, and the effect this has had on the village is clearly seen going down the High Street.

The road follows the valley of the river Ogwen and in 3 miles (4.8 km) crosses over the A55 expressway. In front, at the next roundabout is the entrance to Penrhyn Castle. Built in the nineteenth century as a neo-Norman edifice, it is the result of fortunes made by the Pennant family firstly from sugar in the West Indies and later from the vast quarry in Bethesda. Now owned by the National Trust, it is well worth a visit as an example of Victorian excess.

The road now drops down into Bangor with Port Penrhyn to the right. Keep to the road up to the station with the University buildings on the right and the Cathedral, older than Canterbury, is on the left. As a shopping centre it is not particularly well endowed, and most of the shops are on one long street which runs parallel to the main road. There is a car park down to the left at the mini-roundabout.

Keep on the main road round the one-way system, keeping to the right of the station on what used to be the A5 but is now the A5122. The road curves round the University area of Upper Bangor and there is a viewpoint on the right looking down on the northern end of the Straits. Continue to the roundabout by the Antelope Hotel and take the second exit to cross over the Menai Suspension Bridge.

Built in 1825 by Thomas Telford, as perhaps the greatest challenge on his road from London to Holyhead, the bridge was designed for the horse-drawn vehicles of the day, but apart from replacing the wrought iron chains with steel in 1936, the original bridge carries today's traffic. It is 1,000 feet (300 m) long with a central span of 579 feet (170 m) and is 100 feet (31 m) above high water.

Go ahead at the first roundabout and at the second turn left on the A4080. Just over a mile (1.6 km) along this road is a lay-by from which there are magnificent views of the bridges and Strait with the Snowdon mountains in the background.

The road leads to that famous village with the ridiculously long name invented by a local to drum up business, but known as Llanfair Pwllgwyngyll. Apart from the name it is home to the Marquis of Anglesey at Plas Newydd (owned by the National Trust) whose ancestor, the first Marquis, lost a leg at Waterloo whilst acting as Wellington's aide. The tall column, with 115 steps, at the start of the village was erected in his honour. In 1915 the first Women's Institute in the country was established here. There is also a popular retail outlet.

Instead of carrying on to the village take the slip road on the left onto the expressway and over the Britannia Bridge. The original box girder bridge was built by Robert Stephenson in 1850, to carry the railway across the Strait, thus linking London to Holyhead by rail, but it was destroyed by fire in 1970. It was replaced by the present single arch bridge, with the expressway carried above the railway, thus relieving the suspension bridge of the heavy commercial traffic.

Leave by the first slip road and at the roundabout beneath take the third exit to pass under the roadway and go straight ahead at the next ⇨ Caernarfon. The high wall on the right marks the boundary of the Faenol estate built by the Assheton-Smith family out of the proceeds of their vast quarry in Llanberis. The products of the quarry were brought down by rail to a purpose-built harbour (Y Felinheli) on the Strait.

At the roundabout at the foot of the hill take the second exit onto the Felinheli by-pass and at the far end roundabout go straight ahead for a couple of miles (3.2 km) back to Caernarfon.

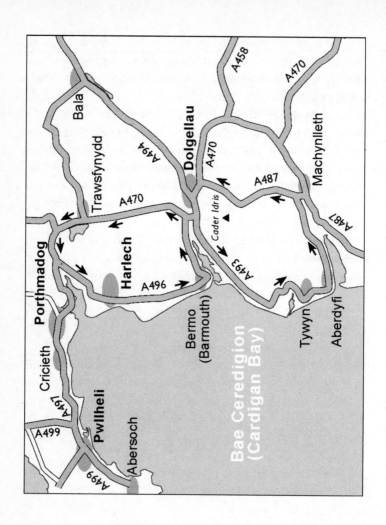

2. Southern Snowdonia National Park

Description

We start from Porthmadog, the town developed by William Madocks, who built the mile-long embankment, thus reclaiming several thousand acres of land and establishing it as a major port for the slate industry. Proceed along the Cob (embankment) shared with the Ffestiniog Railway and follow the A487. After a mile, in Minffordd, is the entrance to Portmeirion, the fantasy village built by the well-known architect Clough Williams-Ellis: worth a visit, despite the admission charge, to view the fascinating collection of buildings set beside the beautiful Dwyryd estuary. There are shops, cafés and hotel.

A little further on is the headquarters of Parc Cenedlaethol Eryri (The Snowdonia National Park).

At the entrance to the next village, Penrhyndeudraeth, take the road to the right of the church ⇨ Harlech Toll, to join the railway and cross the rather rickety toll bridge over the Dwyryd. On the left just before the bridge are the remains of the explosives factory, which, along with quarrying, provided employment for the village.

Shortly after the bridge, turn right on the main A496 to pass through the hamlet of Talsarnau and then when the main road turns sharply to the right continue on what now becomes the B4573. In three miles (4.8 km) enter Harlech. The well-known castle is another that Edward I built in 1290 to reinforce his hold on Wales. In a strategic position perched on a rock overlooking Bae Ceredigion (*Cardigan Bay*) it could be supplied from the sea, but despite this it was captured by Owain Glyndŵr in 1404 and served as the military centre of his revolt. It was recaptured in 1408 and held for the Lancastrians during the Wars of the Roses, giving rise to the song 'Men of Harlech'. It was the last Royalist stronghold in

Britain to fall to Parliament in 1647. The sea no longer laps its walls, and is separated from the castle by the Royal St David's Golf Course and a wide magnificent beach. There are plenty of shops and cafés.

The next significant village is Llanbedr, where the road to the east leads up the beautiful river Artro to Cwm Bychan and the river Cwmnantcol. Salem chapel is at the start of Cwmnantcol. The chapel was made famous by the painting of a Welsh woman taking her pew, which was used in an advert for Sunlight soap; the original hangs in the Lever Art Gallery.

Further up this valley is the birthplace of John Jones, brother-in-law of Oliver Cromwell, who signed the death warrant of Charles I. (He himself was later executed.) The road down to the right leads, past what was RAF Llanbedr, to Ynys Fochras (*Shell Island*) (only such at high tide), noted, naturally, for its shells and camping site.

Leaving the village is Maes Artro Tourist Village with several attractions for young and old. It is now a straight 7-mile (1.2 km) run down the A496 to Bermo (*Barmouth*). *En route* is the village of Dyffryn Ardudwy, where there are several Neolithic burial sites just to the east of the road, and, next, Tal-y-bont, where there is a museum of Old Country Life. There are a number of large caravan sites along this road, fortunately mostly hidden below the road.

Entering Barmouth turn right ⇨ Traeth (beach) just before the pedestrian crossing and follow the street, over the level crossing, onto the promenade where there is plenty of parking. This holiday town, tucked in between the sea and a steep hillside, developed with the arrival of the railway in the late 1800s, its wide expanse of sand and beautiful situation being the attraction. The church above the town was founded on Worcester Sauce, and Dinas Oleu, on the cliff behind, is the first property to be acquired by the National Trust in 1895. The attractive harbour has a lifeboat museum and an unusual small, round lock-up to house drunken sailors and gold miners! If time permits, a short stroll along the toll bridge gives a wonderful view up what is considered by some to be the finest estuary in Wales, the Mawddach.

The road now follows the northern bank of the estuary, with views across to Cader Idris, passing through the hamlet of Bont-ddu, above which is the Clogau gold mine, the traditional source of Royal wedding rings. This is gold mining country and the hills are pockmarked with old workings. All the mines are now closed as uneconomic, but apparently there is still gold there. Turn right onto the A470 in the hamlet of Llanelltyd, cross the new bridge over the Mawddach and shortly turn left on what has now become the Dolgellau by-pass ⇨ Dolgellau and in just over 0.5 mile (800 m) turn right to enter Dolgellau. There are toilets and a car park on the right.

This bustling market town, with its close proximity to Cader Idris and easy access to Coed-y-brenin and the Mawddach, is a favourite with walkers. It has a close association with the Quaker movement, whose members settled here before being forced to emigrate to America. A stroll around the market square is a good excuse for a coffee in one of the many cafés. Following round the one-way narrow streets leave from the south-west corner of the square alongside the market hall ⇨ Tywyn and in a mile (1.6 km) join the main A493.

This attractive road runs between the Mawddach estuary and the foothills of Cader Idris and after 9 miles (14.5 km) come to the village of Friog where, down to the right is Fairbourne, a settlement largely of retirement and holiday bungalows. There is a miniature railway running out along the spit of land opposite Bermo to where a ferry operates in summer. The road now climbs sharing the cliff edge with the railway and giving good views down over Abermaw and across the bay. The next village is Llwyngwril, where there is little of interest except an old Quaker burial ground and the remains of a small Iron Age fort. Next is Llangelynnin, with a tiny church almost on the shore. The road now turns inland to drop down to the river Dysynni. Three miles (4.8 km) up this valley will be seen a high rock outcrop, this is Craig yr Aderyn (*bird rock*), the only inland site in Britain where cormorants nest, a reminder that the sea once flooded this valley. There are many choughs here too. In the village of Bryncrug the road turns right and then there is a straight run into Tywyn.

Follow the streets round the one-way system, passing the interesting church and the ornate Assembly Rooms next door, down the main street to pass under the railway onto the promenade, where there is ample parking.

Tywyn was developed as a holiday resort in Victorian times by John Corbett, a salt magnate from Droitwich Spa. Its main attractions are the miles of glorious sands and the narrow gauge Tal-y-llyn Railway. The railway has been in continuous service since its inception in 1867 to bring slate down from the Bryneglwys quarry 7 miles up the Dysynni valley, to the main line.

In 1914 Marconi established the first commercial radio transmitter directed to America, at Waunfawr, near Caernarfon and to receive messages back built another station here in Tywyn. The stations were closed down just prior to the last war. At the end of the promenade the road turns inland to shortly rejoin the A493 at the Talyllyn Railway station and museum.

Turn right, and in just over 4 miles (6.4 km) enter Aberdyfi where there is ample parking on the sea front. Once a fishing and trading port exporting slates, wool and oak bark for tanning, it is now a pretty little holiday town. Across the estuary is the Ynys Las National Nature Reserve and just beyond the popular holiday village of Borth. There is an excellent golf course and facilities for sailing (the GP.14 dinghy was first adopted here). The Outward Bound scheme was founded here during the war, and the centre provides youngsters with a rigorous experience of all outdoor activities.

The road now follows the beautiful Dyfi estuary and the first significant village is Pennal, where the church is of interest and the, hardly visible, remains of a Roman Fort on the banks of the Dyfi. Three miles (4.8 km) further on join the A487 ⇨ Dolgellau and carry straight ahead (the road to the right, over the Dyfi bridge, leads, in just under a mile [1.6 km] into the market town of Machynlleth where Owain Glyndŵr established, in 1404, Wales's first Parliament.

Keep to the main road as it follows the river Dulas through the Dyfi Forest, and after a couple of miles (3.2 km), in the tiny hamlet of Pantperthog, there is a minor road on the right that leads across the valley to the Centre for Alternative Technology, an internationally known centre demonstrating the use of wind, water and solar power.

Just under 3 miles (4.8 km) further along the main road is the quarrying village of Corris down in the valley. The quarries have gone, leaving a pretty little village where enthusiasts are restoring the narrow gauge railway. A little further on is a Craft Centre with individual craft shops, café and toilets. Here too it is possible to take a boat trip inside the mountain.

Beyond the slate tips of Corris Uchaf the road drops down to Minffordd where the road comes in from the attractive Tal-y-llyn lake, and from where the shortest and steepest route up Cader Idris starts. The 2,928 ft (893 m) mountain, whose name translated means 'chair of Idris' dominates the view in front. The road now climbs steeply for 2 miles (3.2 km) to Bwlch Llyn Bach – there is a lay-by near the top with a fine view back down the valley to the lake. Descending for 2 miles (3.2 km) join the main A470 road at the now closed Cross Foxes Hotel and turn left for the 3 mile (4.8 km) descent to Dolgellau, which is by-passed.

The A470 follows the Mawddach valley into the vast Coed-y-brenin (*King's forest*), so named to commemorate the Silver Jubilee of George V. The next small village is Ganllwyd, where there is a car park, also toilets and picnic area down by the river. Across the road a short walk up a rough track through the forest leads up to the spectacular Rhaeadr Du. This is gold mining country, and at the Forestry Commission Visitor Centre, 2 miles (3.2 km) further on, there is an exhibition locating the old mines and the method of extraction as well as information on the many miles of tracks through the Forest. There is parking, toilets and café.

The road now leaves the forest for a long straight stretch. The views to the left are of the Rhinog Mountains. On the opposite, at Bronaber, is a holiday village and artificial ski slope on what was a big army camp.

In the village of Trawsfynydd there is a bronze statue commemorating Ellis Evans, 'Hedd Wyn', the local boy who was awarded the Bardic Chair for his poetry five weeks after he was killed in the first war. The village is by-passed. The largely artificial lake of the same name was created to supply water to the hydro-electric station in Maentwrog, but later was mainly used to supply the first inland nuclear power station at the northern end of the lake. The station, designed by Sir Basil Spence to blend into the landscape, came on load in 1965 and is now in the lengthy process of decommissioning. There is a visitor centre and nature trail.

Shortly after the entrance to the power station a minor road on the opposite side leads up to Tomen y Mur, the remains of a Roman Fort and Amphitheatre, and Sarn Helen, the Roman road heading south. Shortly after, the A470 goes off to the right to Ffestiniog but our route carries on, becoming the A487 to drop down to Maentwrog. Crossing the Dwyryd it rises slightly and bears left by the Oakley Arms, to reach Penrhyndeudraeth and then back over the Cob to Porthmadog.

Glossary
of a few Welsh words

At this point a note on the pronunciation will no doubt be helpful. To speak and write in Welsh as with all languages requires a certain amount of dedication and study, but to be able to pronounce the place-names is relatively easy. Unlike English, Welsh is a phonetic language – with only one sound represented by each letter. Once the 'sound' and 'letter' are connected in the mind, pronunciation is simple.

Take *Cymru* (Welsh for 'Wales'), for example. The 'y' is pronounced as a 'uh' and the 'u' as 'ee'. The double 'dd' is similar to 'th' (as in 'those') and the 'w' as 'oo'. The difficult one is the 'll' the nearest to which is 'kl' (with a rather soft 'k'). The single 'd' and 'l' are as in English, whereas the single 'f' is a 'v' and the double ff as 'ff'. In common with languages other than English, Welsh puts the noun before the adjective, i.e. Tŷ Coch translates as Red House: 'tŷ' being 'house'.

aber	river mouth
afon	river
bach	little
bryn	hill
bwlch	pass, col
cae	field
caer	fort
capel	chapel
carreg	stone
cefn	ridge
coed	wood, forest
craig	rock
croes	cross

cwm	valley
dinas	fort
du, ddu	black
ffordd	road
ffynnon	well
heddlu	police
isaf	lower
llan	church land
llyn	lake
maen	stone
maes	town square
mawr	big
moel	bare mountain
morfa	sea-marsh
mynydd	mountain
nant	valley
newydd	new
penrhyn	headland
pentre	village
pistyll	waterfall
plas	mansion
pont, bont	bridge
porth	harbour
pwll	pool
sarn	causeway
stryd	street
traeth	beach
tŷ	house
uchaf	upper
ynys	island
ysbyty	hospital
ysgol	school

A brief list of important dates in Wales' history

Ice Age	The Ice Age sculptured the landscape of Snowdonia as we see today
Stone Age	Numerous burial chambers around the coast. Stone axe factories at Penmaenmawr and Mynydd Rhiw
Bronze Age	Copper mined on the Great Orme 1860 BC
	The Iron Age Settlements on Tre'r Ceiri, Garn Boduan and other hills
100 BC	Druid stronghold on Anglesey
AD 43	Romans arrived
AD 51	Caradog, the Brythonic leader, lost to Claudius
AD 60	Paulinus invades Anglesey to subdue Druids
AD 77	Agricola builds string of forts to keep control
AD 394	Romans depart
AD c.400	Cunedda founded the kingdom of Gwynedd
AD 546	St Deiniol founded Bangor Cathedral
AD 784	Offa built his dyke
1170	Prince Madog set sail to discover America
1194	Llywelyn Fawr became king of Gwynedd, and later unified Wales
1198	Geraldus Cambrensis, historian, appointed Bishop of St David's Cathedral
1240	Llywelyn died
1246	Llywelyn ap Gruffudd took over kingdom, and later became Prince of Wales
1277 Treaty	He surrendered land and powers to Edward I following of Aberconwy
1282	Llywelyn ap Gruffudd murdered by the English at Cilmeri
1284	Treaty of Rhuddlan. Edward I built a string of castles for his invading forces but faced many Welsh revolts
1400	Owain Glyndŵr led revolt against Henry IV and attacked or captured colonial castles in Wales
1404	Owain Glyndŵr called national parliament at Machynlleth and crowned Prince of Wales by the first democratic gathering in Wales
1415	Revolt petered out
1536	Act of Union; Welsh language outlawed
1586	First Welsh book printed on the Little Orme